UNDERSTANDING BLACK ADOLESCENT MALE VIOLENCE

Its Prevention and Remediation

AMOS N. WILSON

First Edition
Fourth Printing

Typesetting and Editing by SABABU N. PLATA

Cover design by Joseph Gillians

Special Thanks to Adisa Makalani

ISBN 1-879164-03-5

AFRIKAN WORLD INFOSYSTEMS
743 Rogers Avenue, Suite 6
Brooklyn, New York 11226
Http://www.ominara@aol.com

Printed in the USA

UNDERSTANDING BLACK ADOLESCENT MALE VIOLENCE

Its Prevention and Remediation

A MOS **N.** W ILSON

New York 1992
Afrikan World InfoSystems

Dedication

To my son Raaheem

Other Books by Amos N. Wilson

The Developmental Psychology of the Black Child

Black-on-Black Violence: *The Psychodynamics of Black Self-Annihilation in Service of White Domination*

Awakening the Natural Genius of Black Children

The Falsification of Afrikan Consciousness: *Eurocentric History, Psychiatry and the Politics of White Supremacy*

Blueprint for Black Power: *A Moral, Political and Economic Imperative for the Twenty-First Century*

About the Author

Professor AMOS N. WILSON is a former social caseworker, supervising probation officer, psychological counselor, training administrator in New York City Department of Juvenile Justice, and Assistant Professor of Psychology at the City University of New York.

Born in Hattiesburg, Mississippi, in 1941, Amos completed his undergraduate degree at the acclaimed Morehouse College in Atlanta, Georgia. He later migrated to New York where he attained his Ph. D. from Fordham University in New York City.

Familiarly referred to as Brother Amos, he availed himself for numerous appearances at educational, cultural and political organizations such as the First World Alliance, the Afrikan Poetry Theatre, Afrikan Echoes, House of Our Lord Church, the Patrice Lumumba Coalition, the Slave Theatre and CEMOTAP to name just a few. His travels took him throughout the United States, to Canada and the Caribbean. Dr. Wilson's activities transcended academia into the field of business, owning and operating various enterprises in the greater New York area.

CONTENTS

Introduction

We are all familiar with the crime statistics — the explosively escalating number of homicides among Afrikan American inner-city youth; with the trafficking in cocaine derivatives and their violent, socially devastating side effects on Afrikan American communities across the land; with the virtual reign of terror in our streets perpetuated by relatively small but menacing gangs of youths, muggers, robbers and thieves; with the appalling waste of the "young, gifted and Black."

We will therefore not repeat twice-told tales in this volume. We will however attempt to offer a preliminary outline of some of the most important causes of the phenomena of Black male adolescent criminality. This task was undertaken not in an attempt to "explain away" or rationalize the misbehavior of Black delinquent youths, particularly violent youths, but to provide a causal analysis of Black adolescent criminality which will permit a host of practical solutions to the problems it represents.

In this volume we present what may be called an "interactionist" explanatory approach to understanding the causes of Black male adolescent criminality in many of America's ghettos. Unlike the standard obscurantist, defensive, question-begging, one-factor explanations offered by Eurocentric criminology which predictably ends up blaming the victims — and recommending their lengthy incarceration and/or execution — we offer herein a multi-causal explanation, the implications of which if appropriately translated into educational, rehabilitative, social and institutional reorganization, would move us beyond blaming to resolving.

The resolution of problems of criminality, drug trafficking and abuse, of academic, occupational and social failure of too many Afrikan American inner-city youth while

1

not instigated by the Afrikan American community, must be initiated and executed by that community. While these problems must be borne and ultimately resolved by the whole of the nation, by both White and Black America, it is incumbent on the Afrikan American community, its scholars, leaders and members to arrive at a consensus concerning their causes and to become a unified and effective social-political catalyst for their solution. The text of this volume presents a suggested causal analysis which in no way claims to be complete, totally veridical or definitive but which may help to provide a basis or foundation for construction of theoretical and workable approaches to drastically ameliorating and preventing much of the youthful antisocial and self-defeating, self-destructive behavior which plagues our communities today.

Our thesis is that Black male adolescent criminality is the principal outcome of (1) White-on-Black violence which in its many varied forms, began with the enslavement of Afrikans and has continued unrelentingly to this very moment; (2) the fact that Black male criminality, whether alleged or actual, is a deliberate creation of White American-dominated, race-based society and serves a political, sociopsychological and economically necessary role in maintaining that society[a]; (3) and the unrelenting and the collective ego-defensive and politico-economic needs for White America, to criminalize, denigrate, and degrade Black America.[b]

We further hypothesize that the White American racist need to perceive Black Americans as socially, morally, behaviorally and intellectually inferior, in addition to being innately criminally inclined. Expressed as a continuous and tireless media campaign assault on the character of Afrikan

---

[a] For a fuller explanation of this proposition and how it is actualized in Black-on-Black violence, please read *Black-on-Black Violence* by the author.

[b] Ibid.

people, history and culture, creates and sustains a false, misdirected, aversive state of consciousness in the Afrikan American community. This state of consciousness interacting with the negative social and material conditions under which White racism forces Black Americans to live, makes many Afrikan American youth, particularly inner-city, poverty-stricken youth, vulnerable to antisocial behavior. Furthermore, we contend that the ordinary crises common of adolescence, which represent extraordinary crises for Black youths in the ghettos of White America, interact with historical and contemporary White-on-Black violence and racism, and the uniquely negative socioeconomic conditions maintained by the White-dominated racist status quo, to literally drive many Afrikan American male adolescents pell mell into the clutches of criminality.

Our thesis, however, does not rest the case of Black male adolescent criminality at the feet of White American communal perfidy and leave it there while the Black American community helplessly implores the heartless White American political-economic establishment to resolve its especially life-threatening problems not of its own making. For having been thrown into a hole the Afrikan American and Afrikan world communities must climb their way out under their own initiative and power.

We believe that the recommendations we suggest in the relevant section of this volume, if appropriately and vigorously implemented, provide some doable, effective, deterrent and preventative means for dealing with the problems of Black male adolescent criminality and antisocial conduct. It lies within the Provence and power of the Afrikan American community to implement them. The recommendations are by no means exhaustive or fully detailed, merely suggestive. We do not pretend to have the answers. These must be provided by the Afrikan American community itself. We only hope our attempts herein make some contribution to the solution and not to the problem.

Amos N. Wilson

3

CHAPTER 1

Origin and Impact of Adolescent Black-on-Black Male Violence

The following discussion provides an outline delineating the major causes of Black-on-Black violence among male adolescents. The scope of the present volume does not permit a fully narrated discussion of the many variables which confluently determine Black-on-Black violence. The outline below is meant to suggest the role the Afrocentric curriculum can possibly play in alleviating the plague of violence which is devastating the lives and futures of large numbers of adolescent Black males and vitiating the viability of many Afrikan American inner-city communities. The continuation and increase of adolescent Black-on-Black violence threaten the ultimate survivability of both the Afrikan American and Pan-Afrikan communities. The psychodynamics of Black-on-Black violence, its politico-economic function in the United States, and the threat it represents to the viability of the Afrikan American community is detailed by the author in another book, *Black-on-Black Violence: The Psychodynamics of Black Self-Annihilation in Service of White Domination.*

White-on-Black Violence

Violence is a form of social interaction, a type of social relationship. It is rooted in social history and represents a type of proaction and reaction relative to that history. Violence occurs in a social-historical-cultural context and cannot be divorced from it. Essentially social in its origins, nature and outcomes, criminality, its rates, prevalences and social locations reflect the socioeconomic, sociopolitical dynamics of the society of which it is a product. Crime and interpersonal violence do not originate and have their being in a societal vacuum. They are therefore genetically rooted in society. A society such as American society which breeds a very broad variety and extraordinary quantity of criminality and violence, whether they characterize the society as a whole or some identifiable segment of it, may arguably and justifiably be referred to as a "crimogenic society," a society which breeds unusual numbers and types of criminals and a relatively high level of crime and violence. Therefore, the origins of Black-on-Black violence in America are rooted in and reflective of the sociocultural, politico-economic past and contemporary history of America. Black-on-Black violence speaks not primarily to social relations between Blacks, even though that is of ultimate importance, but to the nature and complexity of the social relations between Whites and Blacks in America and in the world. Black-on-Black violence reflects to a very significant extent the violent origin of America as a nation, the past and contemporary history the violent interactions between White America and Black America. The violence of White America directed toward Black America, both overt and covert, physical and psychological, political and economic, social and cultural, is the violence that begets the largest measurable portion of Black-on-Black violence.

The failure of social scientists to examine Black-on-Black violence and criminality in the context of White-on-Black violence and White criminality in general, has led to the serious misinterpretation of the causes of Black-on-Black violence and Black criminality. It has led to the stereotyping of Blacks, especially young Black males, as innately criminal. There is a need for the dominant elements of White America to maintain their pristine self-image, to perceive

6

themselves as faultless and superior to Afrikans whom they oppress and exploit.

The need by Whites to maintain their highly positive self-perception compels them to deny, distort and rationalize their past criminal and immoral behavior toward Afrikans in America and their current complicity in maintaining the vast majority of Afrikans Americans in conditions of stifling subordination; to project stereotypical images onto Blacks as innately inferior in intellect, character and morals, and on the young Black male as innately crime-prone. Furthermore, this stereotypical perception of Blacks has not only led to "blaming the victims" of White-on-Black violence, but, more importantly, to regressive, social, political, economic, "correctional" and "rehabilitative," educational, social welfare, legislative and administrative policies and practices, which not only have failed to remediate or ameliorate the problems of violence and criminality both within and without the Afrikan American community, but actually have exacerbated them.

EuroAmerican society has an original and unbroken history of violence against its Afrikan inhabitants. This society had its violent origins in the near-decimation of native peoples, the theft of their lands and resources, the enslavement of Afrikan peoples and theft of their dignity, identity, culture, humanity, along with their economic productivity and inalienable right to be free. The physical and psychological violence of White America against Black America which began with Afrikan slavery in America has continued to this moment in a myriad of forms: wage slavery and peonage; economic discrimination and warfare; political-economic disenfranchisement; Jim Crowism; general White hostility and Klan terrorism; lynching; injustice and "legal lynching," the raping of Black women and the killing of Black men by Whites which have gone unredressed by the justice system; the near-condoning and virtual approval of Black-on-Black violence; differential arrests, criminal indictments and incarceration of Whites and Blacks, etc.; segregation; job, business, professional and labor discrimination; negative stereotyping and character assassination; housing discrimination; police brutality; addictive drug importation; poor and inadequate education; inadequate and often absent health care; inadequate family support, etc. This list should make us mindful of the fact that American society is crimogenic, particularly with regard to Afrikan American adolescent and young adult males, not necessarily just because of its criminal and immoral origins — not because of what may be called its "original sins." For original sins can be atoned for, restituted, reparated and forgiven. American society can be described as crimogenic because it *denies* its commission of these sins, and to add insult to injury, attempts to rationalize and justify its sinful behavior toward Afrikan Americans by impugning and slandering their ethnocultural origin and character, blaming them for their socioeconomic, sociopolitical oppression, and by continuing to actively oppose their inherent right to be free, self-defining and self-determining.

Community Effects of Black Male Homicide

According to a report by the Secretary's Task Force on Black Minority Health (1985), homicide is the primary cause of death for Black males between the ages of 15 and 34. The U.S. Department of Justice (1987) reported that in 1986 Blacks accounted for 44 percent of all murder victims. Between 1978 and 1987, the average annual homicide rates for young Black males were 5 to 8 times higher than for young White males; 4 to 5 times higher than for young Black females; and 15 to 22 times higher than for young White females (*The New York Times*, 1990). During this period of time, some 20,315 young males were killed. Some 78 percent of these homicides, 15,781 Black male homicides, involved the use of firearms.

Citing statistics provided from a report on Black male homicide compiled by the Federal Centers for Disease Control (Robert Froehlke, principal author), *The New York Times* (1990) reported that the homicide rate among Black males is "rising fastest among those ages 15 to 19, indicating that violent death [is] becoming increasingly a problem among adolescents." In 1987, homicides among Black males accounted for 42 percent of the deaths of males between ages 15 to 24. Quoting Robert Froehlke of the Federal Centers for Disease Control, *The New York Times* (1990) reported the following information:

> In some areas of the country it is now more likely for a black male between his 15th and 25th birthday to die from homicide than it was for a United States soldier to be killed on a tour of duty in Vietnam.

Citing evidence presented by Rosenberg and Mercy (1986), and Dietz (1987), Bell and Jenkins (1990) indicate that "it has been estimated that for every completed homicide, there are 100 assault victims." Bell and Jenkins further indicate some of the "staggering" emotional and economic costs to the Afrikan American community entailed by Black-on-Black violence and homicide. They include the following results:

- The loss of many men prior to or just entering into their prime years of work and family development.

- The loss of prime productive years by the perpetrators of homicidal acts and the lowering of the social status, marketability and employability of ex-offenders, thereby increasing their chances of continuing their homicidal and violent activity.

- Accelerating the already declining male-female ratio thereby distorting the structural characteristics of the Black family, and impairing its socioemotional and economic health as a consequence.

- Emotional pain and scars which may emotionally skew the lives of the survivors of the victim and the relatives and friends of the perpetrator as well.

- Emotional, behavioral and residual emotional disturbances, e.g., symptoms of post-traumatic stress.

- The emotional and behavioral disturbances and residual emotional scars, e.g., symptoms of post-traumatic stress experienced by the victim's survivors and in some instances, disturbances resulting from the witnessing of violence by children who are relatives, neighbors, friends of the victim or innocent bystanders who happen to be children, may contribute to cycles of family and intragroup violence.

- Random violence serves to maintain a tone of terrorism, states of chronic stress, suspicion and paranoia in inner-city communities.

- Fear of and loss of faith in Black youth.

- Isolation and economic disinvestment of the inner-city communities thereby helping to bolster criminality.

- The institution of a virtual police state, semi-perpetual martial law and concentration-like camp atmosphere in many inner-city communities.

- Invasion of schools and other social institutions by violence or fear of violence.

- Loss of hope, the instigation and maintenance of personal and social apathy and incipient hostility.

The Psychosocial Aftereffects of White Racism

The list of White people's attacks on Black people is long and dreary. It is this list of continuing White-on-Black violence which for the most part breeds the psychological states and psychological attitudes, relations and behaviors which under certain circumstances further lead to Black-on-Black violence in many of its various shades, gradations and forms. Historical and contemporary forms of White-on-Black racism and violence induce and maintain in varying degrees the following psychological states in all Afrikan Americans.

Chronic Anger — ranging from overt, barely controlled, easily-triggered rage to profoundly repressed, over-compensated even-temperedness, passivity and submissiveness.

Chronic Frustration — resulting from being prevented from reaching desired and important goals due to a wide range of obstacles put in place by White-dominated society or from knowing or sensing that their ability to reach desired goals can be arbitrarily inhibited or facilitated by dominant Whites — that their destiny rests inordinately in the hands of Whites. Reactions to frustration may be expressed in a broad variety of ways, e.g., anger; fear; aggressiveness-overt, passive, and/or displaced; apathy (learned helplessness); dependency; regression; depression; fantasy; lowered aspirations; substitute satisfactions; emotional and intellectual insulation.

Chronic Conflict and Ambivalence — Love-hate relations with and attitudes toward Whites are internalized as love-hate conflicts within themselves as individuals and as a

11

community. Chronic conflict and ambivalence also result from the personal, social, political and economic contradictory representations, demands, values, choices, and dilemmas which come with being Black in racist White America.

Displaced Aggression — Provoked to aggressive anger by the White American community and the White American/ European imperialistic establishment, by-and-large, the Afrikan community has contained the expression of its aggressive anger within itself, not directed it at its true sources and causes. This "displaced aggression" expresses itself in many forms in the Black community — horizontal or Black-on-Black violence; various forms of self-depreciation, depreciation of other Blacks, self-defeat, self-narcotization, self-destruction, disruption and/or destruction of the social and physical environment and widespread social rebelliousness, particularly among the youth. Displaced aggression may also be represented as general apathy, indifference and withdrawal or compulsive hedonism.

Internalization of Racist Attitudes — Many in the Afrikan American community having been misinformed, misdirected and miseducated by their White American oppressors and having arrived at the mistaken conclusion that their suffering is caused by their blackness, their being perceived as different by their White oppressors — and not caused by the psychopathology of White racism — internalize white racist stereotypes of themselves and attempt to deny their ethnicity by identifying with and/or imitating the behavior and attitudes of their White oppressors. Internalization and imitation are potent sources of Black mutual disrespect, Black internal communal conflict, Black-on-Black violence, Black self-alienation, self-hatred, self-abnegation of various types. They are also potent instigators of class divisions and disunity within the Afrikan American community. This is especially the case when the middle and upper classes of that community are irresistibly attracted toward the way of life of their White oppressor counterparts and share an overpowering aspiration to assimilate with them.

Chronic Sense of Threat, Vulnerability and Anxiety — conditioned by a long history of unprovoked, irrational, egregious White hostility and physical abuse, official abuse (e.g., police brutality), psychological abuse; surrounded by Whites and other ethnic groups who are known to harbor unfriendly, hostile, suspicious attitudes toward them due to their social status in American society; and not knowing under what circumstances these attitudes may be overtly or subtly expressed, induces and maintains a chronic, often unconscious sense of threat, vulnerability and anxiety in Blacks. Threat involves the anticipation of harm, rejection or humiliation — reactions highly associated with white-black social encounters.

Ego-defense Orientation — The unrelenting need to protect against the aversive situations and conditions listed above; to protect against self-devaluation, emotional hurt, loss of confidence, anxiety, physical harm and to meet the contradictory adjustive demands of being Black in White America, tends to stimulate in Afrikan Americans the construction and intense use of ego-defense mechanisms. Defense mechanisms involve the use of fundamentally unconscious processes by which a person defends himself against threat and anxiety by distorting reality or denying the existence of certain relevant aspects of it and by engaging in some form of self-deception.

Compensatory Striving — Related to the ego-defensive orientation described above, this orientation often occurs

13

in Blacks in reaction to feelings of inadequacy, rejection, low status, unattractiveness generated by White racism by disguising, denying or counterbalancing these feelings by intense social climbing, intense striving for social acceptance and prestige, personal over-achievement, striving to identify with their oppressors. Additional compensatory reactions may include the oppressive-compulsive emphasizing of and striving to attain socially desirable or valued traits and the consuming of items in order to cover feelings of inadequacy, social overconformity, extreme religiosity or their opposites, extreme nonconformity and amorality.

Relative Powerlessness and Fatalism — White power advantages and socioeconomic domination, Black power disadvantages and socioeconomic subordination, "perverse White paternalism" and Black dependency, imply too many Blacks that their fate is not in their own hands, but the hands of their White oppressors. The White-Black power differential potently breeds Black fatalistic attitudes toward their situation — the belief that they are powerless or that their power is relatively limited by White authority relative to resolving their problems. Lacking penetrating insight into the very human nature of their White oppressors and the fragility of their system of oppression, deceived by racist propaganda, many, if not most Blacks, harbor an almost mystical belief in the absolute power, invulnerability, invincibility and immortality of their White oppressors.

Consumer Orientedness — Reduced to the socioeconomic role of wage-earners, cheap and surplus labor, "hewers of wood and carriers of water," the only other role position left to Blacks by the White owners of "the means of production" and service organizations is that of consumers. Through mass media manipulation and political propaganda, the need to exhibit social status symbols and to compensate for feelings of inadequacy resulting from social marginality as well as sociological necessity, Blacks too frequently over-consume and come to view consumption as an end in itself. The consumer-orientedness of Afrikan Americans compounds their problems of unemployment, poverty, the nonexistence or non, or relatively weak, functionality of vital social, economic, political, cultural, educational institutions. This further reduces Black political power and influence and engenders strong tendencies toward political-economic disorganization and social-political economic disunity.

Restricted and Conflicting Affectionate Relations — Having internalized White racist perceptions of themselves, perceptions which lower their self- and social-esteem, very large numbers of Blacks are prone to host various conflicts, distortions and fears regarding affectionate attitudes and relations among themselves. This does not imply that Blacks are incapable of love and affection, and that Blacks do not demonstrate these states and relations. This certainly is not the case. However, it is arguable that these states and relations must be so relatively constricted, tenuous, limited in scope, or conflicted or troubled by their oppressive existence, that they do not gain the unifying sociopolitical and economic potency which would permit the Afrikan American community to collectively overthrow its White American oppressors. Because high levels of love for family and race, high levels of social, political, economic coopera-tion, reliability, mutual trust and responsibility among Blacks are inimical to the continuity of White domination, White disinformation and negative propaganda, economic machinations must operate "overtime" to vitiate or function-ally restrict fully viable Black affectionate and cooperative relations.

15

Stress — The psychosocial effects of White racism described above combine to produce and maintain chronic levels of conscious and unconscious stress in Black Americans. Depending on a number of other personal and social factors, stress in the Afrikan American community ranges across a spectrum of relatively mild to extremely severe and life-threatening social, psychological and physiological disequilibrium and disease.

Adolescent Crises of Inner-city Youth

To the psychological outcomes of White-on-Black violence listed above, which are pervasively present in Afrikan American society and culture and in individual Afrikan American personalities, must be added the special psychological and subcultural outcomes generated by adolescence, in general, and Black adolescence, in particular. The transitional nature of adolescence is problematic for Afrikan American adolescents particularly as they struggle to define themselves and find their way in the confusing and distracting context of an oppressed, exploited Afrikan American community and a dominant, hostile, racially oppressive and exploitative European American-dominated society. The forbidding complexity of this situation as represented in the self-perceptions, world-views, attitudes and behaviors of Black adolescents may, in interaction with a number of other personal, valuational, familial, social and economic factors, lead to Black-on-Black violence (including violence against the self).

The factors which characteristically and generally define adolescence in America and which, when represented in the collective personality of Black adolescents, interact with factors related to " being Black in White America," include the following:

16

- The effort to resolve critical issues concerning self-identity (including ethnic identity), sexual, gender and social identities.
- Efforts to establish and maintain self-esteem (for males — masculinity); efforts to deal with issues revolving around the acceptance and rejection of social norms, adult and parental values and demands, adult authority and control.
- Body image; self-consciousness and self-confidence.
- Emotional liability, i.e., moodiness; boredom; confusion about life, its meaningfulness and purpose and a sense of direction.
- Social acceptance and popularity relative to the peer group.
- General feelings of alienation; anomie; powerlessness; need for attention.
- Vocational and career choices and possibilities.
- Intellectual, cognitive/behavioral development and prowess.
- Issues revolving around status symbols — clothing; hair styles; body adornments; automobiles; money and invidious comparisons of the self with others, race and nationality.

Socioeconomic Context of Inner-city Youth

The critical issues of adolescence as they are uniquely represented in Black adolescents, especially Black male adolescents within the context of the Afrikan American community, encircled as it is and in many ways negatively influenced by the European American community, do not necessarily lead to adolescent Black-on-Black violence. Whether such violence occurs, depends of how the issues of adolescence are dealt with and resolved. However, the methods by which Black adolescents, the resolutions of the crises faced by Black adolescents and the outcomes which flow from them, are heavily influenced by the general psychosocial orientation common to the Afrikan American community which are reflective of that community's experience in America and more important, by the contemporary socioeconomic arena in which Black adolescents carry out their struggle for survival and fulfillment.

The same or similar adolescent concerns and critical issues are coped with and resolved by different means and with different outcomes during different periods of time; depending on different environmental, political, economic, familial, communal, and sociocultural circumstances, class and family backgrounds; religious commitments or ethical/value orientations; levels of income; levels of education; residential location; personal competencies (i.e., "intellectual abilities, social and physical skills and other special abilities" (Atkinson, et al., 1987); long-term expectancies and personal ability to plan and regulate self-behavior. All these factors combine to interact with the foregoing sociohistorical factors, adolescent crises and the factors listed below (the contemporary social-economic context) to determine the negative, or positive, or mixed attitudinal-behavioral outcomes observed in Black adolescents. Where the characteristics just mentioned tend to be inadequate, impaired and generally negative, the attitudinal-behavioral outcomes also tend toward the incompetent, inadequate, maladaptive, illegal, criminal, or violent end of the personal-social spectrum.

Today's Black adolescents, particularly poverty-stricken, un- or under-employed, inadequately educated, alienated Black male adolescents, exist in a socioeconomic, sociopolitical world drastically different from that of their parents, especially of their grandparents. The causes of Black-on-Black adolescent violence can only be garnered from including in a causal equation the interactive relationship between Afrikan sociohistorical relations with White

America, their effects as reflected in the collective sociopsychological orientations which characterize the Afrikan American community, the adolescent crises with which Black adolescents must contend, and the contemporary socioeconomic, sociopolitical, sociocultural and ecological contexts within which these crises must be resolved for better or for worse. The contemporary context which surrounds many inner-city Black adolescents includes some of the following characteristics:

- High levels of adult and adolescent unemployment, poverty and overcrowded, inadequate, often unhealthy living conditions.

- Very inadequate preschool, primary and secondary school education; inadequate job-training facilities and preparation.

- An overwhelmingly segregated urban existence.

- A post-modern/industrial/de-industrialized world.

- A world where data and information processing is becoming the basic industry of America in contrast to its factory-based, labor-intensive past where poorly educated, uneducated, unskilled persons and school dropouts could find employment. This catchment or safety net essentially no longer exists.

- A world of television and mass marketing, advertising specifically designed to evoke consummatory desires and artificial needs in adolescents and children.

- A time of rising expectations (with an increasing poverty of means of fulfilling them).

- A time of family dissolution (the characteristic single-headed Black family of current renown began after the 1960s).

- A time of conservative, if not hostile, governments on national and state levels.

19

- A time of dramatic demographic changes in the American population and changes in the power and economic relations in the world.

- An inner-city world characterized by the absence or dysfunctionality of vital sociocultural, socioeconomic institutions which can deal appropriately with the demands of the 21st century.

- An inner-city world which in many instances resembles a police state or which has been ignored and abandoned to its self-destruction by the government and unconcerned citizens.

- A world of armed, violence-prone, hedonistically oriented, delinquent, criminally inclined gangs and peer groups.

- An urban world flooded by addictive drugs, infectious diseases, firearms of all sizes, types and power.

- An urban, national and international market which provides little room for Black manufacturing, wholesaling, retailing, service or professional activity.

CHAPTER **2**

Sociopathy and Psychopathy

The sociohistorical origins of America, the generally negative
sociohistorical and contemporary relations between White
and Black America and their pervasive effects on the
psychosocial orientations or tendencies and material
conditions of Black America, the relative absence or
inadequacy of personal/competencies and communal
institutions and organizations, the subcultural context we
just described, interact to induce in many Black adolescent
males a state of consciousness which lends itself to hysteria,
impulsivity, dyssocial and sociopath-like behavior. There
exists a general tendency for the dominant elements of
White America to utilize their power and influence to
inculcate these tendencies in Afrikan Americans in order
to maintain the effectiveness and efficiency of their
dominance. It is in the Black-on-Black violent adolescent
that we see so dramatically expressed, the successful
inculcation of these tendencies.

In the context of today's Black urban ghettos, Afrikan
American youth, unprotected by a firm Afrikan-centered
identity and consciousness, unguided by a deep and abiding
sense of higher purpose, untutored and untrained by strong,
independent Afrikan-centered family and cultural institutions, are prone to fall victim to a series of projective,
political and economic assaults on their personalities,
perceptions and perspectives which predispose many of them
toward a life of crime and violence. These assaults on the
psyche of these vulnerable adolescents which are but the
aftereffects of the same assaults against the collective

psyches of their ethnocultural group, their class, local community and family are such that many react to them with psychopathic- or sociopathic-like tendencies. These, what we may term "psychopathoid" or "sociopathoid" tendencies are less severe and more remediable versions of the classic psychopathic or sociopathic disorders. A series of definitions of these disorders by various authors will give the reader a "feel" for their essential nature and antisocial implications. As cited by Millon (1969), the *sociopathic personality disturbance, antisocial reaction* refers to:

> . . .chronically antisocial individuals who are always in trouble, profiting neither from experience nor punishment, and *maintaining no real loyalties to any person, group, or code.* They are frequently callous and hedonistic, showing marked emotional immaturity, with lack of a sense of responsibility, lack of judgment and *an ability to rationalize this behavior so that it appears warranted, reasonable and justified.* [Emphasis added]

Millon additionally cites McCord and McCord (1964) as describing the psychopath or sociopath in the following manner:

> His conduct often brings him into conflict with society. The psychopath is driven by primitive desires and an exaggerated craving for excitement. In his self-centered search for pleasure, he ignores restrictions of his culture. The psychopath is highly impulsive. He is a man for whom the moment is a segment of time detached from all others. His actions are unplanned and guided by his whims. The psychopath is aggressive. He has learned few socialized ways of coping with frustration. The psychopath feels little, if any, guilt. He can commit the most appalling acts, yet view them without remorse. The psychopath has a warped capacity for love. *His emotional relationships, when they exist are meager, fleeting and designed to satisfy his own*

desires. These last two traits, guiltlessness and loveless-ness, conspicuously mark the psychopath as different from other men. [Emphasis added]

Gough (1948) describes behavior characterized as antisocial, psychopathic, or sociopathic in the following way:

[O]verevaluation of immediate goals as opposed to remote or deferred ones, *unconcern over the rights and privileges of others when recognizing them would interfere with personal satisfaction in any way*; impulsive behavior, or apparent incongruity between the strength of the stimulus and the magnitude of the behavioral response; *inability to form deep or persistent attachments to other persons or to identify in interpersonal relationships*; poor judgment and planning in attaining defined goals; apparent lack of anxiety and distress over social maladjustment and unwillingness or inability to consider maladjustment qua maladjustment; *a tendency to project blame onto others and to take no responsibility for failures*; meaningless prevarication, often about trivial matters in situations where detection is inevitable; almost complete lack of dependability of and willingness to assume responsibility; and, finally, emotional poverty.

We italicized portions of above citations to bring attention to those characteristics of sociopathic or "sociopathic" behavior in Black male adolescents which in good part are the result of the White American assault on the collective psyche and material conditions of Afrikan Americans noted at the beginning of this section. This especially refers to results of the projection of negative stereotypes by influential White American media onto Afrikan Americans combined with the other inducible co-factors listed above.

The lack or inadequate knowledge of the tremendously positive sociocultural history of Afrikan peoples, of the testaments to the high intellectual, civil and moral character of peoples of which they are descendants, and the tenuousness, restricted range, or rather low level of self-esteem which reflect these prior conditions, leave many Black adolescents unresistingly open to the internalization of projected negative Afrikan stereotypes and image distortions by the dominant EuroAmerican community. The internalization of negative stereotypes of Afrikan peoples, of themselves, and the internalization of White racist attitudes toward their people and themselves lead to an estrangement, an alienation from themselves as persons and their people as a group.

Internalization of White racist projections onto Afrikan people motivates in many adolescent Black males a conscious and/or unconscious tendency to disavow membership in the Afrikan ethnocultural group; a tendency to "dis-identify" with other Afrikan Americans and — with the exception of family and peers — a tendency to feel a certain amount of contempt, hostility or indifference toward other Afrikan Americans and all things "Black" or Afrikan. These tendencies together operate to effectively destroy or impair any feelings of loyalty to the Afrikan American community, its members, as well as Afrikans the world over. There also may exist no sense of loyalty to the moral codes of the group as well as an actual tendency to directly flaunt or attack such codes. These alienated attitudes and behavioral tendencies predispose some Black adolescents to violently assault other members of the Afrikan American community without a sense of guilt or remorse. As a matter of fact, some may gain a sense of cathartic relief, sense of pleasure or power after having committed an unprovoked assaulted on or having exploited another fellow Afrikan. The tendency to break moral codes, besides possibly reflecting an absence of effective moral training, reflects the fact the violent Black adolescent has witnessed the breaking of such codes without impunity by the larger dominant EuroAmerican community (its ruling classes) while loudly proclaiming its moral superiority to its Afrikan victims. Moreover, these youths have also witnessed the reactive and concomitant breaking of such codes in their family and primary group. The psychological and material gains, the pleasure, power, privileges, prestige and other advantages achieved by the dominant EuroAmerican society and perhaps persons and groups in his community with which he is familiar, through their victimization of Afrikans may serve as potent demonstrations of what is to be gained from the self-serving, self-centered pursuit of one's own satisfactions without regard for the pain to fellow Afrikans such pursuits may cause.

In his perception of the hypocritical behavior of the dominant EuroAmerican community toward the Afrikan-American community — the former abusing and exploiting the latter in every possible way and then blaming the latter community as responsible for its own victimization; rationalizing its anti-Black attitudes and behaviors in terms of defending itself the alleged depredations of the latter community thereby denying any responsibility for its actions — the Black-on-Black violent adolescent may find a model for rationalizing his own psychopathological behavior toward other Afrikans and then blaming them for their own victimization by him.

The reactive internalization of negative EuroAmerican attitudes toward themselves; rationalizing his own pathological behavior in ways imitative of the anti-Black rationalizations of the dominant EuroAmerican group; accepting the self-serving rationalizations of his delinquent peers help, the Black violent adolescent to shape his own rationalizing tendencies, his tendencies to blame his victims, others and circumstances for his own irresponsible behavior.

The Black-on-Black violent adolescent develops his own victimology in order to justify victimizing others, especially his fellow Afrikans. Based on a reactionary, self-serving biased perception of reality, this violent "sociopathoid" adolescent may exhibit one or more of the following characteristics (based on five characteristic features of the sociopathic disorder, developed by McCord and McCord, 1964, as cited in Millon, 1969).

Disdain for Social Conventions Perceiving the fact that in too many instances racist EuroAmericans, the Euro-American establishment, the authorities, persons and communities which are made to symbolize it act as if the established customs, laws and guidelines which they themselves formulated and approved and which are presented as applying equally to all groups, do not in fact apply to themselves in their relationships to the AfroAmerican community or to any of its constituents, the adolescent sees no reason why he should follow the rules either. This attitude is doubly reinforced when the disdain for social conventions is flaunted by influential role models or peers.

Deceptive Facade Having intuited that the dominant EuroAmerican society and its AfroAmerican imitators, "despite their disrespect for the rights of others, . . .present a social mask, not only of civility but of sincerity and maturity" (Millon, 1969), the criminal or violent Black adolescent sees no good reason why he should not "con" and manipulate his fellow Afrikans order to reap the same benefits as those he has chosen to imitate.

Inability or Unwillingness to "Adjust" Following Punishment. Millon (1969) intimates that "many sociopaths are of better than average intelligence, exhibiting both clarity and logic in their cognitive capacities. Yet they display a marked deficiency in self-insight, and rarely exhibit. . . foresight [regarding] the implications of their behavior. The habits and needs to abuse and exploit Afrikans are so deeply rooted in the EuroAmerican psyche, that the racist attitudes and behaviors toward Afrikan Americans on the part of EuroAmericans are relatively impervious to reasoning, moral suasion, demonstrations and punitive reactions on the part of the AfroAmerican community. Such actions on the part of the latter community are themselves deemed by the EuroAmerican community as unreasonable, unfair, intimidating and intended to do harm to or victimize it. The criminal, violent Black adolescent uses the same or similar effective technique to feign innocent victimization by those he victimizes and thereby establishes a new "justification" for continuing his irresponsible attitudes and behaviors. This scenario may also be paralleled within the context of the adolescent's own socially reactionary primary group.

Impulsive Hedonism Witnessing the single-minded pursuit of treasure, pleasure, adventure, power and advantage by EuroAmericans (as presented in their myths, legends, media productions and history books as well as daily life), their acting as if they were immune from danger; misperceiving the short-sighted, foolhardy behavior of members of his primary group, the criminal or violent adolescent likewise perceives this approach as "idea" for handling his low tolerance for frustration, delay of gratification, boredom, and for providing himself with one exciting and momentarily gratifying escapade after another. This especially applies when his access to such sources of gratification is owned or blocked by persons for whom he has little or no respect, for whom he feels contempt, who are perceived by him as undeserving and/or weak or vulnerable.

Insensitivity or Disregard for the Feelings of Others The seeming incapacity for EuroAmericans, particularly their political leaders and representatives, to share tender feelings, to experience genuine affection and love for another [especially outside their ethnocultural group, i.e., AfroAmericans] or to empathize with the needs and distress of others — the seeming pleasure many EuroAmericans appear to gain in the thought and process of hurting others [e.g., AfroAmericans]; in seeing them downtrodden and suffering pain and misery; often go out of their way to exploit others; and yet not be punished or otherwise chastised or penalized for the distress and pain they leave in their wake but seem to enjoy all the more the tangible fruits of their cunning and deceit; to see the fruits even multiply — leaves an almost indelible impression on the would-be criminal Black adolescent. When these examples set by the larger, dominant EuroAmerican society are successfully duplicated by the adolescent's neighborhood role models it becomes exceeding difficult to convince him that insensitivity or disregard for the feelings of others does not provide its own abundant and readily available rewards, that crime does not pay.

The victimology of the sociopathoid individual, i.e., his rationale for perceiving himself as victim rather than a perpetrator or victimizer, is based on his restricted and rather paranoid perception of himself as being victimized by others who themselves exhibit a disdain for social conventions; engage in deceptive and hypocritical practices; seem to act without compunction and to perceive any penalties levied against them for even the most obvious or egregious misconduct towards others, as unfair and as a basis for continuing the misbehavior or as a basis for revenge; who evidence a single-minded pursuit of pleasure or need satisfaction without regard for the painful effects such pursuit may have on others — while forbidding him the same privileges and rights. Thus, the sociopathoid personality is motivated by a deep and abiding sense of and sensitivity to real or perceived unfairness or injustice to obtain his due by any manipulative means necessary. He is an aggrieved person. His grievances whether alleged or actual or some one-sided, exaggerated combination thereof, provide the foundation for his intentional, insensitive abuse and exploitation of others, for his suspension of the Golden Rule.

The reader must note that we are not referring to violent Black adolescent males as psychopaths or sociopaths. We have attempted to demonstrate here how intergroup relations, e.g., between EuroAmericans and AfroAmericans, where one group possesses inordinate power compared to the other and the more powerful group, project negative stereotypes on the weaker, often dependent group, directs overtly and covertly hostile attitudes and behaviors toward the weaker group, and abuses its power over the latter group — may under certain conditions induce attitudinal and behavioral orientations in members of the subordinate group which to a limited degree resemble some of those exhibited by extreme or "classic" psychopaths or sociopaths.

The "classical" or typical sociopath is a deeply and pervasively disturbed personality who generally "tends to be a "loner," with no genuine loyalty to anyone or anything, lacking the power to share and feel affection toward others . . .[whose] behaviors are often foolish or purposely aggressive, enacted without apparent rhyme or reason" (Millon, 1969). The behavioral orientation we have labeled "sociopathoid" which while sharing the sociopath's disdain for social conventions along with a number of the other sociopathic characteristics pointed out above is more similar to "dyssocial reactions" which, according to Millon "are stimulus-specific responses to circumscribed conditions, usually. . .learned as a consequence of faulty past experiences, these experiences did not permeate the entire fabric of the individual's personality make-up." Millon goes on to indicate that "dyssocial reactions are seen most commonly in group delinquency behaviors and in planned criminal activities." Our "psychopathoid" or "sociopathoid" reaction while certainly not as intensely psychopathically severe and pervasive as the psychopathic or sociopathic reaction, is significantly less benign than is the dyssocial reaction.

Sociopathoid behavior is the product of painful experiences resulting from rather specific types of familial-primary group relations, inadequate socialization experiences inside and outside the home (schools and other cultural institutions), occurring during early childhood and the witnessing, observation, or intuitive understanding of how the abuse of power, cunning, misuse of advantage and opportunity, deception and the single-minded, insensitive pursuit of self-centered goals and ambitions, can be utilized to attain both highly desired material and nonmaterial rewards which under any other circumstances would apparently not be available. The reactions to painful, distorted social relations and inadequate socialization experiences, to the witnessing or imagining of the one-sided abuse of advantage for selfish gain, manifest such *mis*perceived traumatic potential that the sociopathoid individual finds it necessary to reject his real self; to repress empathetic identity with his ethno-cultural group, pledge allegiance to its "flag"; to repress normal human sensitivities and normal conscience; and to alienate or estrange himself from the more humane and sensitive inner core of his personality, for fear that if he were to claim his true self and ethnocultural identity — to lift his repressions and come into contact with his true feelings — he would suffer psychological and possibly physical impoverishment, vulnerability, disorganization, or annihila-tion. Yet it must be kept in mind that the central causal nexus of psychopathoid or sociopathoid reaction or disorders in low-socioeconomic class, inner city Black males is the alienation from their Afrikan identity, consciousness and self and the alienation from an Afrikan-centered community (which they have in common with all other Afrikan American classes) and society in general, brought on by unrelenting, vicious, full variety of assaults against his Afrikan heritage, community and people by hostile and self-serving White imperialist ruling and managing classes.

Black-on-Black violence is by far most likely to occur when alienation of many inner-city males combines with impulsive (i.e., short-sighted, labile, volatile), hysterical (i.e., impressionistic, diffused, distractible) and dyssocial (i.e., peer and/or gang-oriented, *manifestly bent-on disregarding accepted social and moral codes*) orientations which are stimulated and reinforced by the socioeconomic conditions under which they live. Yet we must be ever mindful of the fact that this type of alienation and these maladaptive orientations along with the psychosocial conditions which synergistically conspire to coalesce them into aggressively self-destructive and socially destructive forces, are themselves sociopolitically and socioeconomically instigated and maintained by a self-serving, self-centered upper and ruling class regime. However, such a regime can only hold sway over Afrikan Americans and Afrikans in general as long as their consciousness and identity are not Afrikan-centered.

CHAPTER 3

Black Adolescent Masculinity
and Antisocial Behavior

While lack of space will not allow us to cover this important matter sufficiently, we must mention that a goodly portion of Black male violence against other Black males is the consequence of unresolved conflicts around masculinity. The resolution of what it means to be a man is a major crisis of adolescence and young adulthood under normal circumstances, how much more the case for the Black adolescent and young adult male under conditions of oppression.

It is well known that the males of a captive or oppressed people are the targets for special and more intense oppression by their captors and oppressors than are their oppressed female counterparts. This is the case simply because their principal captors and oppressors, usually males themselves, expect greater and more nakedly aggressive resistance to their dominance from captive and oppressed males. While not denigrating the resistance and revolutionary roles played by women under oppression, we think that the psycho-historical record will reveal that the freedoms, movements, social assemblies and activities of oppressed males which may be perceived by their oppressors as possibly empowering their abilities to resist and overthrow their masters, are subject to acute surveillance and repression. As an important part of protecting themselves against overthrow and maintaining the effectiveness of their physical, psychological and socioeconomic security and dominance, maintaining high levels of masculine self-esteem, self-concept and self-confidence, oppressive males attempt to undermine the physical, psychological and socioeconomic stability and security of oppressed males. Moreover, they undermine and destabilize the masculinity of oppressed males by minimizing their self-esteem, negating and destroying their self-concept, self-perception, their self-confidence, or by severely restricting the development and expression of these factors in ways which would liberate them from their oppression. In a word, the oppressed male is ideally made and kept "nonthreatening" to the oppressive regime of his oppressive male counterpart. The relationship which we have sketched, despite appearances to the contrary, is fairly descriptive at this juncture of the relationship between the oppressive EuroAmerican male and the oppressed Afrikan male in the world today, extending back some several centuries in the past.

In spite of their oppressive conditions Afrikan American males have sought to develop a masculine ideal, a cultural model of what it means to be a man. The approximation of this ideal under the aegis of the oppressive White male regime by the vast majority of Afrikan American males has been remarkable. From their oppressed ranks have emerged generation after generation, from the time of their very captivity in Afrika and enslavement in the New World to this very moment, men who have risen to challenge their oppressors and helped to push back the frontiers of oppression. There have been others who under the most discouraging of circumstances have fed and protected their families and communities and who have contributed their genius to expanding the material, civil and cultural development and prosperity of their people.

Yet there also has been and is too large a minority of Afrikan American males whose immaturity; whose reactionary frustration to the restrictions placed on their masculine possibilities and to the obstacles placed in the way of achieving what they had been told represents the achievement of masculinity; whose training for positive manhood is nonexistent or inadequate; whose avoidance of masculine responsibility or confusion about what it means to be a man under oppression, have moved them to accept an incomplete, distorted, self-defeating and, sometimes, self-destructive definition and expression of masculinity. These males, often misguidedly and ignorantly assuming that they are successfully defying White male authority and dominance, defying "the system," expressing their independence and "masculine prerogatives," expressing their "manhood," have been misled or misdirected into violently attacking and corrosively undermining the peace, stability, and the very viability of the Afrikan American community. These males have been provoked by their oppressive circumstances into what we may call a "reactionary masculinity" whose presence and expression are essentially detrimental to the Afrikan American community and, ironically, to their own well-being.

Characteristics of Reactionary Masculinity

- Lacks a sense of social responsibility or social interest.
- Lacks a deep and abiding Afrikan identity and consciousness; exhibits an impoverished empathy for others.
- Tends toward rigid and excessive self-interest, self-centeredness, self-service, intolerance, stubbornness.
- Tends to be opinionated and to view every social encounter as a test to his masculinity, as a struggle for power.
- Mistakenly identifies physicality, crudeness, with masculinity; views domination, insensitivity, uncon-cern, willingness to injure or kill, seek revenge, as essentially masculine traits.

- Motivated primarily by fear, avoidance, escape, retreat from responsibility, ego-defense, and reactionary frustration; by a deep and ever-present sense of inadequacy; by an inferiority complex; and an obsessive need to appear superior.

- Perceives cooperation with other males, submitting to the rightful authority of other males; conceding "points" to other males and relating to them, as humiliating insults to their masculinity.

- Believes the mastery of knowledge, crafts, academic subject-matter, professional expertise, the actualization of intellectual potential, to be essentially feminine.

- Is a conspicuous consumer; consumer-oriented — concerned mainly with parasitically exploiting others, works merely to earn "spending money," i.e., money to spend irresponsibly; is "into" flashy clothes, cars, fads, and styles of all types.

- Motivated and defined by self-alienation; exhibits an absence of self-knowledge; ignorance of his ethnic-heritage; unbounded hedonism; narcissistic drives; deep insecurities regarding the reality of his masculinity and of his masculine courage.

- Lacks self-control, discipline, persistence, and high frustration tolerance; lacks long-term goals and commitment to prosocial values.

Note: The following list of characteristics is derived and quoted from Adler, in Ansbacher & Ansbacher (1956)

- Typified by defensive and compensatory intent, impudence, courage, impertinence, inclination toward rebellion, stubbornness, and defiance, accompanied by phantasies and wishes of the role of a hero, warrior, robber, in short, ideas of grandeur and sadistic impulses. The inferiority feeling finally culminates in a never-ceasing, always exaggerated feeling of being slighted. . . .

- They are attacked much more by the difficulties of life and feel and live as though they were in enemy country . . .They are therefore selfish, inconsiderate, lacking in social interest, courage, and self-confidence because they fear defeat more that they desire success.

- They consider other people enemies. Later in life they are not adapted for occupation, love, marriage, because they consider only their own welfare and are not looking for the interests of others. Sometimes they turn toward crime, and they are, in childhood, the majority of the problem children.

- They feel curtailed and behave like enemies. They use their strength only if they are stronger, sometimes in a cruel manner against weaker persons or animals. . . .It is difficult to win them and to develop social interest and courage to do useful work.

- For the safeguarding of [their] picture of the world and for the defense of [their] vanity, [they erect] a wall against the demands of actual community life. Without clearly realizing it [themselves], they exclude or shove aside all disturbing problems of life, while they abandon [themselves] utterly to their feelings and to the observation of [their] symptoms.

- They see everything with the eyes of [their] vanity. They approach every situation and problem of life with fearful anticipation as to whether [their] prestige will be assured. . . .

- If [their] vanity is offended, [they] react with cold disdain, marked ill-humor, or downright aggression [Reich, 1970].

- The meaning [they] give to life is a private meaning. No one else is benefitted by the achievement of [their] aims, and [their] interest stops short at [their] own person. [Their] goal of success is a goal of personal superiority, and [their] triumphs have meaning only to themselves. . . . A private meaning is, in fact, no meaning at all.

- [When a criminal they]. . .always look for excuses and justifications, for extenuating circumstances, and for reasons that "force" them to be criminal.

- [Their criminality] is a coward's imitation of heroism. Criminals think they are courageous; but we should not be fooled into thinking the same. *All criminals are actually cowards. They are evading problems they do not feel strong enough to solve. . . .He feels himself incapable of normal success. . . .He hides his feelings of inadequacy by developing a cheap superiority complex.* [Emphasis added]

- [They] regard the partner in love merely as a piece of property, and very often [they] thinks that love can be bought. It is something [they] ought to possess, not a partnership in life. [**Note:** End of quotes from Adler].

- They exhibit essentially what is referred to in psychoanalytic theory as a "phallic character" or "phallicnarcissistic character." Phallic characters are persons whose behavior is reckless, resolute and self-assured — traits, however, that have a reactive character. They reflect a fixation at the phallic level, with an overvaluation of the penis and confusion of the penis with the entire body. This fixation is due either to a castration fear [i.e., a fear of failure as a man, fear not being a "real man", fear of having his "manhood" destroyed] . . .or to a defense against temptations, toward an analreceptive aggression" [i.e., fear of being forced to submit utterly, of falling completely under the power of another, of being made a symbolic passive, homosexual by another man or a "sucker" by a woman] (Fenichel, 1945).

- They measure their manhood by the number of sexual conquests they achieve and the number of children they have sired (in contrast to the number for whom they have assumed paternal responsibility and economic support). They thereby exploit both women and children and help to disfigure and maladapt the family structure, impoverish women, children and communities, and contribute to social dysfunctionality in various forms, including criminalization of the next generation of males.

- They find no deep satisfaction on any level of activity and are forced into continued pursuit and conquest (Lowen, 1958). Therefore, their relationship with women tends to be exploitative, fleeting, unstable, disloyal and unreliable.

- Unconsciously, the penis, in the case of the male of this type, serves less as an instrument of love than as an instrument of aggression, wreaking revenge upon the woman. . . .In the case of the male representatives of this type, the mother is very often the stricter parent, or the father died at an early age or was not married to the mother and was never present (Reich, 1972).

- In their marital relationships they do not "question the belief that the man should always be strong and superior and that the woman should be weak and in need of leadership." The role of the wife is to confirm his masculinity and success (Willi, 1982). This demand in the face of their obvious subordination and failure to achieve true independence when perceived consciously or unconsciously by their partner operate to destabilize or sabotage their relationship or to maintain the relationship in terms of collusive deception and mutual false consciousness. □

Again we wish to notify the reader that the above-listed characteristics do *not* characterize the large majority of Black males. These traits are most likely to take root and grow in the psyches of young Afrikan American males when they are compelled to live within the "socioeconomic context of inner-city youth" described earlier, and when they are not countered or neutralized by positive family conditions, effective cultural and educational institutions, positive personal-social experiences and relations, and personal competencies. In the absence or inadequacies of the requisite experiences, knowledge, competencies, values and perspectives provided by family, social relations, community and cultural institutions, these males have in common personal constructs of masculinity, implicit theories of what it means to be a man, and concepts of masculine prerogatives whose concrete expression under conducive conditions may lead to academic underachievement, scholastic misconduct, truancy, dropping-out, apathy, vocationally/occupational inadequacy, maladaptive male-female relations, criminality, orientations toward violence, substance abuse and addictions of various types.

However, in the instances of Black adolescent and young adult male delinquency, criminality, and violence masculine immaturity, misperceptions of what it means to be a male or a man, ill-formed definitions and anti-social expressions of masculinity are readily apparent and rather dramatic. This may also be the case in regard to male-female relations, marital and family relations as well. But this does not at all imply that the models of manhood and masculinity demonstrated by law-abiding, fully employed, better educated, trained or skilled, family-oriented and even moral/ethically astute Afrikan American males and men are complete and maturely adaptive. The successful struggles by Black males to maintain the stability of the Black family and community, to advance Afrikan American civil rights and civil liberties, political and economic enfranchisement, educational and occupational interests within the context and confines of White male dominance and racism are to be commended. Within the context and confines of White male dominance and racism however, the failure of "mature" Afrikan American males to assume full responsibility for educating and training Afrikan American boys and adolescents for productive manhood — their failure to take economic and political control of their national communities; to aggressively move in and capture economic territory, real estate, health and other economic institutions in the larger society and the world so as to alleviate and prevent the conditions of which we speak in this volume; their failure to learn of the realities of power and of power relations between groups and nations; to prepare for the defense of Afrikan peoples against their current and future enemies; their willingness to continue their dependence on the largesse of White males; to submit to the dominance of White males in America and the world; their apparent inability, lack of will or courage to form a nation-within-a-nation and to set as one of their ultimate goals the collapse of White male power advantages; their relative powerlessness to transform the social and economic misfortunes of the Afrikan American community and of the Pan-Afrikan community — glaringly reveal their inadequate preparation for assuming the responsibilities of Afrikan manhood, whether they may be classified prosocial or antisocial, responsible or irresponsible.

The fate of a man, his job, social status, civil rights and liberties, and his family is ultimately tied to the fate of some social group or groups to which he relates. These things can only have meaning and be supported by and within some group context. Personal achievements, in the final analysis, are not individual achievements — but group achievements. Therefore, the preservation of the group, of the fundamental society, is synonymous to preservation of the self. Individual Afrikan males, free-standing Afrikan families and isolated

Afrikan communities cannot idly stand by and watch the Afrikan American masses and Afrikan world communities suffer and perish without themselves also encountering the same fate. For those who either through benign neglect or malignant concern would destroy the so-called Afrikan American "underclasses" and the "underdeveloped" Afrikan nations principally because they are Afrikan in ethnic composition or because of their relative defenselessness, would not ultimately hesitate to devour the remaining Afrikan working, middle and working classes and the "developing" Afrikan nations if it were in their interest to do so, and for the very same reasons they devoured the other Afrikan classes and nations. The prevention of these very realistic, possible and ominous eventualities, or to speak more positively, the possibilities for the Pan-Afrikan community to achieve high levels of self-actualization — of realizing its humanistic potentialities and contributing significantly to the true civilizing of America and the world — are intimately related to how the collective Afrikan male defines for himself, what it means to be an Afrikan man in today's world, and how he trains and prepares himself and his sons to realize that definition. Obviously, maleness and manhood are not synonymous. Neither are male adulthood and manhood. Within a cultured context manhood is a conferred status, a socially defined and achieved status. It must be *earned*. Manhood, therefore, involves more than biological maturity, but also includes a special set of social attitudes, behavioral orientations and expressions. A man's self-definition is always, on some level, a social definition. A man lives, and if necessary, dies for his fundamental ethnic or cultural group. Preparations for achieving manhood status may be very formal in traditional societies or informal or rather subtle and somewhat amorphous as in many modern societies. But even in the latter there exist some types of *rites of passage*, milestones, accomplishments or markers, attitudes and behaviors which are generally perceived as masculine and whose existence and expression are seen as necessary to personal and social well-being and stability.

Gilmore (1990) in a cross-cultural study of manhood provides a number of general characteristics and expectations regarding manhood. Some of the conclusions he reached are quoted below.

Cross-Cultural Concepts and Expectations Regarding Manhood

- Regardless of other normative distinctions made, all societies distinguish between male and female; all societies also provide institutionalized sex-appropriate roles for adult men and women.

- . . .manhood ideals make an indispensable contribution both to the continuity of social systems and to the psychological integration of men into their community . . .as part of the existential "problem of order" that all societies must solve by encouraging people to act in certain ways, ways that facilitate both individual development and group adaptation. Gender roles represent one of these problem-solving behaviors.

- . . .the manhood ideal is not purely psychogenetic in origin but also a culturally imposed ideal to which men must conform whether or not they find it psychologically congenial. That is, it is not simply a reflection of individual psychology but a part of public culture, a collective representation.

- . . .there is a constantly recurring notion that real manhood is different from simple anatomical maleness, that it is not a natural condition but rather is a precarious or artificial state that boys must win against powerful odds. This recurrent notion that manhood is problematic, a critical threshold that boys must pass through testing, is found at all levels of sociocultural development regardless of what other alternative roles are recognized.

- The data show a strong connection between social organization and production and the intensity of the male image. That is, manhood ideologies are adaptions to social or psychic fantasies writ large. The harsher the environment and the scarcer the resources, the more manhood is stressed as inspiration and goal. This correlation. . .does indicate a systematic relationship in which gender ideology reflects the material conditions of life.

- Because of the universal urge to flee from danger, we may regard "real" manhood as an inducement for high performance in the social struggle for scarce resources, a code of conduct that advances collective interests by overcoming inner inhibitions.

- For [many cultures, e.g.,] the Masai [and] the Samburu [both East Afrikan tribes], the idea of manhood contains the idea of the tribe, an idea grounded in moral courage based on commitment to collective goals. Their construction of manhood encompasses not only physical strength or bravery but also a moral beauty construed as selfless devotion to national identity.

- Again and again we find that "real" men are those who give more than they take; they serve others. Real men are generous, even to a fault. . . .Non-men are often those stigmatized as stingy and unproductive. Manhood therefore is also a nurturing concept, if we define that term as giving, subverting, or other-directed.

- But surprisingly, "real" men nurture, too, although they would perhaps not be pleased to hear it put this way. Their support is indirect and thus less easy to conceptualize. Men nurture their society by shedding of their blood, their sweat, and their semen, by bringing home food for both child and mother, by producing children, and by dying if necessary in faraway places to provide a safe haven for their people. □

Cross-cultural studies of manhood indicate that what it means to be a man in a particular culture is derived from the recurrent or ongoing problems of living faced by that culture, the modes of production, social activities and relations perceived as vital for maintaining its integrity and cohesion, and the demands placed on its well-being by external factors and groups. The methods by which boys are trained for manhood, the values extolled as masculine and the cognitive/behavioral characteristics expected of a man, are intimately related to the problems just mentioned.

If the social definition of manhood arrived at and the methods of manhood training do not adequately prepare the males to solve or successfully cope with these problems then their masculinity and its expression will tend to be maladaptive, antisocial and will place the society in serious jeopardy.

In light of the problems of living which must be resolved or controlled by Afrikan American males, e.g., unemployment, underemployment, educational underachievement and inadequacy, male-female and marital-family difficulties, crime, violence, incarceration, and subordination to White male dominance, it should be apparent that there is an urgent need for Afrikan American males and the Afrikan American community to critically reassess, redefine and reconstruct what it means to be an Afrikan man in America and the world today. This new definition of Afrikan manhood must not only be a reactionary one, i.e., based solely on the problems which must be resolved by Afrikan males, but must also be a proactive one, one based on the very positive contributions Afrikan males can make to the community and the world. The new definition cannot be an imitation of their White male counterparts. This is the worst example or model of manhood. In fact, as detailed in Wilson's book, *Black-on-Black Violence*, it is due to the fact that many Afrikan American males internalize the racist attitudes, the egregious and rapacious economic philosophy and approaches, and behavioral orientations of White American and imperialistic European males which account in good part for the high rates of criminality and intragroup homicide and violence in the Afrikan American community.

Moreover, the frustrations of their not being allowed to play the full "masculine role" in their homes and communities, and the racist restrictions placed on their exercise of the same "masculine prerogatives, privileges and powers permitted White American males — facilitate the induction of maladaptive and antisocial behavior in many Afrikan American male youths and adults.

The definition of what it means to be an Afrikan American male must be firmly based on an objective and deep knowledge of the sociohistorical experiences of Afrikan peoples; the psychohistorical relations between Afrikans and non-Afrikans, especially Europeans and White Americans; an unflinching analysis of contemporary social, economic, political, cultural, technological and military realities; and realistic projections regarding what the future holds for how that future may be transformed in the interests of Afrikan peoples.

CHAPTER 4

The All-Male Program or School

To unwittingly imitate one's enemies, to indiscriminately imitate their attitudes and oppressive behaviors; to fail to model one's attitudes and oppressive behaviors to fit one's own circumstances and expectations, is self-defeating and self-oppressing. These are the general outcomes for Afrikan Americans who attend "standard" American schools, establishments designed and managed by their oppressors. The "standard" American school wherein they are unwittingly, indiscriminately prodded to imitate their oppressors, even if "successful" in such institutions, is ill-fitted to their history of oppression and to prepare them for liberation from it. The subjection of the Afrikan American male, who is the special target of hostile White male dominance, to "standard" American education, a major instrument of EuroAmerican socioeconomic supremacy, is tantamount to the genocidal subjection, through him, of the Afrikan American and Pan-Afrikan communities.

Consequently, in recognizing the special problems plaguing the Afrikan American male and the Afrikan American and Pan-Afrikan communities and the failure and inability of American schools as currently designed to resolve or even moderately ameliorate these problems, there has arisen in tandem with the general Afrocentric movement, a movement to design and execute a curriculum exclusively for Afrikan American males. Such a curriculum may be practiced as a special program for males within current coeducational establishments or in separate all-male academies or institutions. Proponents of the all-male programs or institutions argue that the critical situation confronted by Black males and the special needs of these males can best be addressed by special programs or schools.

A number of Afrikan American all-male institutions and programs have already been developed or are in the process of development. The programs may include all-male classes taught by Afrikan American male instructors which stress Afrikan cultural heritage and history. The male instructors serve as role models and are expected to exhibit an empathic understanding of their male students and an ability to cope more successfully with the cognitive-behavioral, attitudinal-emotional problems some of these students may present. These programs also emphasize the teaching of positive values, linking the learning experience to real life problems, the provision of so-called remedial instruction, but more importantly, the provision of a broader and more advanced variety of academic, science and technological subject matter and training classes.

In addition to the cultural-historical, academic-technological, values-oriented emphases, a number of programs and institutions emphasize instructional approaches which are designed to counter specific psychological and psychosocial orientations which are common to Afrikan American students of both genders but which obtain more special and more destructive outcomes when acted-out by males. The approaches also seek to appropriately correct or prevent the development of the maladaptive psychosocial characteristics of the "reactionary masculinity" listed earlier.

The tradition of exclusive male education and training is an ancient and honored tradition in Afrikan societies. This tradition, supported by Afrikan females (who also have the tradition of exclusive female education and training) begins with the recognition as stated by Gilmore that "manhood ideals make an indispensable contribution both to the

continuity of social systems and the psychological integration of men into their community." The recognition of the
integrative importance of the social institutions of manhood
training and masculine ideals is concretely expressed by
the practice transitional *rites of passage* or transitional rites
found in numerous cultures.

These rites refer to more than symbolic rituals and acts
performed to mark changes in social relations and processes.
For example, in the case of males or females or other social
categories these rites may symbolize and certify the
completion of certain special training and preparation to
undertake a new social role and function. In the case of the
male, these rites may socially signify the completion of some
level of training for full manhood or adulthood. "Many *rites
de passage* explicitly aim at effecting in individuals certain
changes in motivation, appropriate to the newly assumed
social roles that are publicly proclaimed by the ritual"
(Wallace, 1970). The training, experiential exercises and
rituals have the marked advantage of clearly indicating to
the individual the end of a particular era in his life and the
beginning of a new one and the role expectations and
privileges attached to the new role. The absence or ambigu-
ity of such demarcations in the lives of certain individuals
or groups may under certain circumstances lead to ambigu-
ities of social identity and social status, to social role
confusion and conflicts, social and psychological immaturity,
sex role diffusion, irresponsibility, reactive masculinity and
antisocial behavior.

Even though post-industrial American society does not
explicitly emphasize manhood training and *rites of passage*,
there still remains certain experiences, social and occupational milestones which are utilized to mark important
transitions in social status and role expectations, such as
between boyhood and adolescence, adolescence and young
adulthood and full adult maturity and old age. With regard

to adolescence and young adulthood some of these points of social demarcation may include completion of high school; accomplishment in sports; acquisition of a valued or prestigious skill, of steady employment; certificates of various types; self-support; entry into and completion of service in the Armed Forces; marriage and parentage; religious conversion; a period of delinquency or rebellion followed by "settling down"; achieving voting age, drinking age and legal adulthood; acceptance of some responsible social position, job, or position of community leadership. Perhaps high school graduation, entry into post-secondary education or training — the acquisition of trade, semiprofessional or professional skills, substantial wage earnings; the ability to be self-supporting or to contribute significantly to family income, marriage and family — still represent certain informal experiences and *rites of passage* which help to define manhood and adulthood and their related role expectations in America today. There exist many other more subtle experiences in and out of school which convey to males expectations regarding masculinity and manhood.

When we examine the points of demarcation indicative of transitions from adolescence to adulthood just mentioned, such as high school graduation, the acquisition of valued employment skills and substantial wage earnings, etc., it is apparent that the failure of many inner-city males to achieve these goals within the expected period of time may lead to one or more of the negative or problematic outcomes centered around definitions of masculinity and manhood.

The degree to which an Afrikan American all-male program and curriculum can provide the intellectual and skills development, occupational preparation, personal and social skills development, moral/ethical and cultural training, sense of meaning and purpose, and positive affirmations of masculinity as well as increase the probability of graduation, Afrikan American males will play a major role in the reformation of the Afrikan American community.

It must be kept in mind that traditional manhood training in Afrikan societies was not only concerned with the mastery of stereotypical manhood skills, especially of warfare and economic modes of production, but also involved training for full participation in the society as adults at all relevant levels of social activity, such as training in the skills of "husbandhood," male-female relations, family-hood, and social responsibility. It also involved the mastery of valued intellectual knowledge, personal and social cooperative and leadership skills. Therefore, the mere separation of males for periods of training and education does not in and of itself imply a training and education of males for chauvinistic and dominant or superior attitudes toward females. As a matter of fact, these separate sessions or periods can be utilized to emphasize those very values, skills and attitudes which evoke a high regard and respect for females, family and community. It is quite apparent at this juncture that the type of co-educational experiences many Afrikan American males have undergone has not and is not achieving these and other desirable and necessary ends.

Many Afrikan American all-male programs or institutions which are in operation or proposed for implementation or institutionalization are centered around the academic and social realization of the Seven Principles of Kwanzaa (the *Nguzo Saba*):

- *Umoja* — Unity
- *Kujichagulia* — Self-determination
- *Ujima* — Collective work and Responsibility
- *Ujamaa* — Cooperative Economics
- *Nia* — Purpose
- *Kuumba* — Creativity
- *Imani* — Faith

As with the multicultural and the Afrocentric curricula, the recency of the development and implementation of Afrikan American all-male programs and institutions does not allow the presentation of statistical and other formal evaluations of their educational outcomes. However, according Spencer Holland, (*Daily News,* Feb. 3, 1991) director of the Center for Educating Afrikan American Males, in the School of Education and Urban Studies of Morgan State University:

> The evidence concerning academic achievement, as well as attendance and behavior, from the Baltimore City Public Schools' demonstration classes at the first, third and sixth grade levels of all boys, taught by men, is very encouraging. Preliminary data show that boys in these classes appear to be faring much better, academically and behaviorally, than their peers from the same communities who are in coed classes.
>
> Evidence from a newly published book, *"Girls & Boys In School: Together or Separate?,"* by Cornelius Riordan (Teachers College Press, 1990) which studied the academic achievement of inner-city African American and Latino students in mixed-sex and same-sex Catholic schools, found that both boys and girls in same-sex schools scored significantly higher on standardized achievement tests than African American and Latino boys and girls in mixed-sex schools.

It is important that Afrikan-centered programs for Afrikan Americans boys begin as early as possible. The negative interracial dynamics between Black and White America in general, and more specifically, the embittered clashes between Black and White males, are highly reflected in the dysfunctional psychological and structural dynamics of the Afrikan American family. These dynamics as they are played out in the Black ghettos of America are often acted out in the aggressive and antisocial attitudes and behaviors of Afrikan American boys as early as the preschool years. Such behavior during this boyhood period is highly predictive of scholastic failure and serious delinquent and criminal behavior during the pre-adolescent, adolescent and young adulthood years.

As cited by Wilson and Herrnstein (1985), Conger and Miller (1966) concluded from a longitudinal study of male delinquency which included an analysis of third-grade school records that:

> By the end of third grade, future delinquents were already seen by their teachers as more poorly adapted than their classmates. They appeared to have less regard for the rights and feelings of their peers; less awareness of the need to accept responsibility for their obligations, both as individuals and members of a group; and poor attitudes toward authority, including the failure to understand the needs for rules and regulations in any well-ordered social group and the need for abiding by them. They both resented and rejected authority in the school situation. Their overall social behavior was less acceptable, not simply with teachers, but with peers; they had more difficulty in getting along with peers, both in individual, one-to-one contacts and in group situations, and were less willing or able to treat others courteously and tactfully, and less able to be fair in dealing with them. In return, they were less well-liked and accepted by their peers. They were significantly less likely than their nondelinquent matches to be viewed as dependable, friendly, pleasant, considerate, and fair.

According to Wilson and Herrnstein (1989) "Teachers' ratings of classroom aggressiveness of . . .boys as early as the age of eight predicted later juvenile and adult crime, violent and otherwise. Glueck and Glueck (1950; 1968) in a highly detailed and comprehensive series of analyses of male delinquency found that whether measured in academic, attitudinal, or motivational terms, delinquents perform less adequately than do nondelinquents. The vast majority, i.e., about 90 percent, have established records of misbehavior prior to age 11. Their misbehavior early in school is not only more frequent, but is generally of a more serious nature than that of nondelinquents. Robins and colleagues (1971) found in a study of Afrikan American school boys that in all cases adult sociopathy was preceded by some type of antisocial acts or symptoms in childhood, the most common ones being theft, "incorrigible behavior," running away, poor school performance, and truancy.

A study which involved 1,027 children in Sweden presented data which suggests that highly aggressive boys when compared to their less aggressive counterparts, are approximately three times as likely to become criminals in their later lives. The more the boys were evaluated as aggressive by their teachers at ages 10 and 13 (i.e., in terms of fighting, defiance, etc.), the more likely they were to have committed at least one felonious offense by age 26. One in three had multiple convictions for serious offenses.

However, there is good reason to believe that the high correlations between early childhood, elementary school-age aggressiveness and adolescent and young-adult criminality on the part of males can be significantly reduced if these males are given special attention and educational and group-dynamics experiences early enough in their lives. Early childhood educational programs designed to enhance academic and intellectual performances are of special importance in this regard. This is the case not only because a plethora of studies has consistently shown an association between academic competence and criminal behavior, but intelligence (e.g., measured IQ performance) as mediated by the school experience is substantially linked to crime (Hirschi & Handelang, 1977; West & Farrington, 1978; Hirschi, 1966). Of particular interest in this regard is the so-called verbal IQ. Low scores on this measure, contrasted with higher performance IQ scores, have been shown to be significantly associated with social competence, moral development, interpersonal maturity and a tendency to break the law (Wilson & Herrnstein, 1989). In light of these associations it seems apparent that effective academically oriented early childhood education instructional strategies coupled with strategies designed to enhance and maintain personal-social competence skills, good group relations, positive self-esteem, self-acceptance and high levels of positive ethnocultural group identity, would significantly reduce later social maladjustment, maladaptive behavior, delinquency and adult criminality. Academically oriented preschool programs, such as the Perry High School Project, have demonstrably improved these outcomes even when lacking a definite Afrikan-centered curriculum. We think the addition or integration of an academic orientation within an Afrikan-centered curriculum would very significantly improve the Perry High School record.

There are a number of group techniques and behavior modification techniques which are and have been developed for helping aggressive boys. These include "pair therapy," which pairs an extremely aggressive boy with one whose friendship stimulates the more aggressive partner to learn friendship, cooperative relations, negotiation as an alternative to violence (Selwan, In Press). Play groups of grade school children which include an especially aggressive boy may also be used to engage the aggressive member in games which foster cooperation, listening to others, making deals, asking questions, helping and sharing (NYT, 1990).[c]

---

[c] *The New York Times*, Thursday, February 1, 1990.

Behavior modification approaches include one that teaches parents to modify or reduce aggressive behavior in their boys through systematic discipline and reward. This approach and similar ones which emphasize operational diagnoses of particular types of aggressive behavior and the prescription of a rather simple series of measurable steps for improving such behavior assume that boys' aggressive and unruly behavior is learned and therefore can be unlearned.

We shall now briefly and broadly outline what Afrikan-centered educational, therapeutic and rehabilitative programs can do to counter the social psychology of oppression as manifested in Black adolescents.

CHAPTER 5

Recommendations

Afrikan-centered Educational Rehabilitation

An Afrikan-centered curriculum includes approaches to countering maladaptive tendencies in school children and adolescents as central to its educational mission. These and related approaches in inextricable conjunction with the Afrikan-centered curriculum's programs for maximizing the intellectual and educational achievement of Afrikan American students; for markedly improving their attendance and reducing their misconduct in school; improving their social and moral/ethical thinking and reasoning; raising their aspirations and expectations, can make the curriculum a major force for minimizing crime and violence and other forms of social malfunctioning in the Afrikan American community and in American society in general.

The larger social, political and systemic problem in American society as a whole, that forms the matrix that gives birth to many of the problems prevalent in inner-city communities, must be addressed at the levels where they occur. This means that Afrikan Americans must continue to press for broad social and cultural changes in American society, changes conducive to the attainment of racial equality, equality of opportunity and achievement, positive interracial relationships and the full remediation of psychological, socioeconomic, sociopolitical and other ills which currently characterize too many Afrikan American communities. The national, state and local governments and their agencies must continue to be pressed to provide fully-adequate family support and child care services, welfare and foster care services, affordable housing; income maintenance assistance; job training and employment training programs; health care and health insurance services; increased yearly childhood and general educational funding; and effective civil and human rights legislation.

On the educational and rehabilitative levels, the focus of Afrikan-centered instructional and psychotherapeutic programs must be the eradication of the "nexus of alienation" in the psyche of Afrikan Americans which reactionarily give rise to the "psychosocial aftereffects" referred to earlier. The operative presence of these psychosocial orientations forms the psychodynamic foundations for the sociopolitical, socioeconomic construction of most of the maladaptive behaviors, including Black-on-Black violence, and the social *dis*eases which impair the mental and material health of the Afrikan American community today. Their presence also must be erased if the Afrikan American and Afrikan communities are to achieve liberation from racial and imperialistic oppression and exploitation. The "nexus of alienation" not only includes alienation itself but also includes the lack of knowledge of the crimogenic nature and operation of American racism and EuroAmerican economic imperialism; the sense of powerlessness; inadequate responses to stereotypical projections; unrealistic and self-destructive desires; internalization of racist attitudes; frustration; displacement; imitation of the aggressor; faulty self-concept; dysfunctional self-esteem; hostility; intellectual, social and personal incompetence; among other stress-producing and misdirective factors.

Broadly speaking, some of the maladaptive psychological predispositions which may motivate Black adolescent males to engage in criminality and violence and some methods for their remediation are noted below.

57

Maladaptive Psychological Predisposition	Suggested Method for Remediation
Alienation	The reclamation of an Afrikan-centered identity and consciousness; learning how to love the self and others; developing prosocial, cooperative and communalistic skills and orientations.
Crimogenic Society	Develop a keen and working knowledge of the ways and means by which American society and EuroAmerican imperialism attempt to inbreed in Afrikan Americans and Pan Afrikans psychological attitudes, behaviors and relations which are self-defeating, self-destructive, and supportive of EuroAmerican oppression; develop the intellectual, personal, social skills necessary to defeat the purposes of the crimogenic society.
Internalization of White racist attitudes towards the self	Construct an efficient perception of reality; develop the analytical ability to critically examine racist distortions of facts, racist myths and to discern malevolent racist intentionalities; develop a deep and working knowledge of the psychology of racism and racist strategies of the EuroAmerican ruling establishment.
Racist Projections	Inoculate with deep knowledge of truth and of Afrikan history and culture; knowledge of the psychology of projection, its purpose and func-

tion, and of the criminal and immoral origins of American society as well as the evils of imperialism; develop deep self-knowledge and highly positive self-concept and a high level of self-esteem.

Frustration

Develop ability to clearly discern the personal and social sources of frustration; develop problem-solving and task orientation — i.e., approaches to solving causes of frustration and frustration prevention; learn how to use anger and aggressive feelings stemming from frustration positively and constructively; develop creativity, mental and behavioral flexibility and resourcefulness; develop social intelligence, skills and competence; enhance coping strategies for dealing with stress.

Sense of powerlessness

Learn that the powerlessness of Afrikans Americans is an illusion; develop the means of discerning the tremendous power within the grasp of Afrikan people; learn what power is, how it is achieved, developed and controlled; learn the strategies and means by which Afrikan peoples may become truly empowered and influential and by which they must wrest power from the hands of Euro-American racists and imperialists, training the youth to develop the personal powers, competencies and skills and to realize the power inherent in ethnic unity and collective action.

Displacement of Aggression	Learn the sociopolitical means by which Afrikan Americans are made to perceive each other as primary enemies; learn to confront fears of discerning the real enemies of the Afrikan race and of challenging those enemies; develop which and how economic, political and possibly military means are chosen and utilized to defeat genuine enemies; develop the recognition of the vulnerability of these enemies, that they can be countered, neutralized and defeated; learn how the displacement of anger and aggressive hostility flowing from race-based frustration and reactionary self-hatred and self-alienation onto fellow Afrikans makes matters worse and is ultimately self-destructive.
Egregious self-defeating, self-destructive desires	Learn a new set of Afrikan-centered values; inculcate deep abiding and long-term cultural and personal goals; learn how desires are "manufactured"and produced by the business-commercial-industrial complex and are stimulated and directed by advertising, publicity and public relations; develop the ability to discern when one's desires are being artificially created, manipulated and exploited and the ability to parry these thrusts; learn of the nature of advertising, mass hypnosis, subliminal suggestion, social conditioning, lies, deception and propaganda; learn how the incompetent coping with the effects of racism and frustration may motivate one to seek

self-defeating, self-destructive and addictive palliatives instead of real solutions; learn to be productive; develop the personal, social and business skills for attaining significant ownership of the means of production on the part of Afrikan Americans and Pan-Afrikans as a means of satisfying their own needs and desires; develop self-control, self-discipline and the ability to delay gratification; learn the nature and consequences of drug and substance abuse.

Imitation of the racist aggressor	Learn the true nature and intent of role models and reference groups which, on close examination demonstrate that if unwittingly and indiscriminately imitated, will lead to self-defeat and self-destruction; learn of Afrikan heroes and heroines who provide excellent and realistic role models; develop a knowledgeable appreciation of Afrikan high culture, art and cultural models; inculcate a deep, strong, Afrikan-centered consciousness and identity and highly positive Afrikan ethos and ideals.
Negative self-concepts and self-esteem	Develop an adequate knowledge of the achievements and contributions of Afrikan civilizations, cultures and heroes/heroines; develop programs which emphasize Afrocentricity, co-operation and supportive social relations, which utilize techniques for affirmation of self and the development of intellectual, social, personal,

61

and occupational competencies which help to raise self-esteem and self-acceptance.

Tendency toward inter-personal violence

Develop conflict-resolution skills; develop empathetic skills, the ability to take various perspectives on problems and issues; learn alternative means of dealing with problems; inculcate the approaches listed above.

CDC Strategies for Crime Prevention

The U.S. Department of Health and Human Services (1992), specifically the Centers for Disease Control (CDC) which is currently developing guidelines for the prevention of youth violence, has made some preliminary suggestions concerning strategies which may be helpful in preventing or significantly attenuating Black male adolescent violence. These strategies, among a longer list of others, include: adult mentoring, conflict resolution, training in social skills, parenting centers, peer education, public information and education campaigns, preschool programs, therapeutic activities, recreational activities, and work/academic experiences.

Adult Mentoring

Mentors are special role models who provide a positive, caring influence and standard of conduct for young people. Mentors provide models for young people who have no models or they offer alternatives to negative role models. Mentors may reinforce positive attitudes or behaviors children are trying to express. Adult models may be teachers, counselors, friends, and confidants, or simply members of the community. . . . The attention and interest bestowed on the youngsters by people who care, enhance the youth's self-esteem, strengthening the adolescent's ability to choose nonviolent methods to resolve conflicts.

Conflict Resolution Education

Classes in conflict resolution are designed to provide students with the opportunity to develop empathy with others, learn ways to control impulses, develop problem-solving skills, and manage their anger. . . .Courses in conflict resolution have been developed for students in both elementary and high schools.

The methods used to teach conflict resolution usually include role-playing of conflict situation and analyzing the responses and consequences to violence.

Training in Social Skills

Teaching young people social skills provides them with the ability to interact with others in positive and friendly ways. . . .Aspects of social-skills training include self-control, communication skills, forming friendships, resisting peer pressure, being appropriately assertive, and forming good relationships with adults. . . . These educational activities can be conducted in schools, day care settings, after-school programs, and youth organizations.

Parenting Centers

Improving parenting skills through specially designed classes for parents can improve how the parent and child interact. The improvement in this relationship may reduce the risk of child behavior problems and subsequent antisocial behavior. Programs targeted toward parents must address the psychological needs of the parents. . . and the stresses and social supports that can either help or hinder the parent's ability to adapt to the needs of the child.

Peer Education

Programs that use students to teach their peers about violence prevention are a powerful force among adolescents and can be used effectively to shape norms and behavior in this group.

Public Information and Education Campaigns

Public information campaigns reach a broad audience and draw attention to an issue as well as provide a limited amount of information. There is a wide range of media available for these campaigns: public service announcements, educational video programs, appearances on public talk shows, posters, brochures, and other print materials.

Preschool Programs such as Head Start

Project Head Start is designed to help children of low-income families develop a greater degree of social competence through developing the child's intellectual skills, fostering emotional and social development, meeting the child's health and nutritional needs, and involving parents and the community in these efforts.

Therapeutic Activities

There are a number of therapeutic programs available for abused children [and]. . .treatment programs [which] target school-age children with special needs, such as emotional disturbances or as substance abuse problems.

Recreational Activities

Recreational activities offer young people opportunities to spend time in a structured and purposeful environment. . . .[A]ctivities that provide outlets for tension, stress, or anger and opportunities for social interactions and constructive problem-solving are important parts of a program with other violent prevention components.

Work/Academic Experience

Student work and volunteer activities that are supported by community organizations have a positive influence on students. Structured job experiences and volunteer activities connect adolescents with supportive adults who act as role models, mentors, and counselors. . . .Students learn what a community is and how a neighborhood functions while learning the roles they play in society.

* * *

The suggested strategies and activities for the prevention of youth violence recommended by the Centers for Disease Control (CDC) are generally and specifically, directly and indirectly, designed to provide children and adolescents with the requisite social, emotional, personal and intellectual skills they need to fulfill their personal potentials and to lead and enjoy productive personal and interpersonal lives. These strategies generally involve modification and reorganization of children's educational and social-interactive experiences in ways which will enable them to prosocially operate in their environments and to achieve their positive life-goals. The CDC has compiled specific programs across the country which utilize specific approaches to adolescent crime prevention. They are listed in the adjoining *Appendix*.

The strategies, therapeutic approaches and methods available for prevention and remediation of youth violence work best when applied prescriptively, i.e., when they are applied to certain homogeneous subgroups of children and adolescents who are predispositionally amenable and especially responsive to a particular strategy, approach or method, or a set or sequence of these treatments (Goldstein, et al., 1980). That is, educational and treatment approaches must be based on a sound and thorough analysis and knowledge of the individual and groups being dealt with and a deep understanding of the range, limitations, strengths and weaknesses of the available approaches and a keen sense of their most likely interactive outcomes.

Remediation of Reactionary Masculinity

We have noted that the adolescent and young adult male's conception of masculinity, of what it means to be a man contribute significantly to their prosocial and/or antisocial behavior. Moreover, we contended that the "reactionary masculinity" of many Afrikan American adolescent males is actualized as delinquent, criminal, often violent behavior. It may also contribute personally and socially unproductive behavior, the exploitative use of others, and to various forms of self-defeating and self-destructive behavior as well. If the characteristics of reactionary masculinity are to be reversed and prevented, then educational, communal and manhood training programs should include as an important part of their programmatic mission the objectives listed below.

- Identify the idea of masculinity with Afrikan-centeredness and consciousness, the idea of Afrikan communalism and a commitment to Afrikan collective goals; a sense of social responsibility and interest.
- Associate masculinity with social service, community uplift and defense; with reason, sensitivity, tolerance, patience, flexibility, creativity, generosity; with productivity, economic self-sufficiency, teamwork, cooperativeness, reliability, trustworthiness, honor and courage; with the ability to attain and maintain feelings of love and intimacy for women, children and other males; with courtliness.
- Encourage males to be motivated by positive drives and to strive for positive goals instead of by negative drives such as inordinate fear, anger, vanity, feelings of inadequacy and inferiority and the need to "prove" masculinity.
- Associate masculinity with self-control, the mastery of knowledge, technique, technology, craft and skills;

with intellectual development, self-actualization and positive interpersonal skills.

- Encourage masculine self-definition in terms of productivity and nurturance instead of conspicuous consumption, parasitic exploitation, and faddish fashions.

- Identify masculinity with self-determination, taking responsibility for personal failures as well as successes; with resisting the too-easy temptation to blame others and extenuating circumstances for one's misfortunes or antisocial behavioral tendencies.

- Resist using avoidance, escape, withdrawal and retreat; evasion and denial, projection of false superiority complex, as methods of dealing with problems and painful, unpleasant or unflattering situations.

- Recognize that sexuality, sensuality and pleasurable excitements are important parts of life and among many of its important pursuits but not the whole life, not its only ends; that these passions can be the byproducts of many other productive, positive personal and social vocations and activities; that the mate is the person of equal value to oneself and is due all the deep respect and consideration, freedoms and privileges one demands for oneself; that children are to be nurtured and cared for and not merely utilized to demonstrate sexual prowess and sexual seductiveness.

- Emphasize that family creation, development and maintenance are very serious undertakings and are not to be entered into lightly or blightly.

Training For Liberation and Independence

The central causal factor of maladaptiveness in the Afrikan American community and the Afrikan world community at this time is White American/European domestic and imperialistic domination. Black male adolescent violence and criminality are but aspects or resultants of this larger factor. White American/European domination destroys in Afrikan peoples, especially inner-city Black youth, the sense of mastery over their fate, a key element for attaining and maintaining psychological health, personal and social competence. Dependency bred by domination, the feeling of not being in control or of having a say over what happens in their personal and community lives; feelings of relative powerlessness and the overwhelming desire to achieve a sense of power and control by self-defeating and antisocial means, particularly in the adolescent and young adult male, manifest themselves in ways which adversely affect the physical and mental health, holistic and occupational achievement, social and sexual attitudes and relations of Afrikan American youths and young adults. Black-on-Black violence is one of the critically negative manifestations of an absence of a sense of control bred by oppression.

In essence, our foregoing discussion implies the common-sensical conclusion that feelings of power, competence, mastery, self-control, self-determination and autonomy are of central importance in positive mental health and prosocial behavior. The reasonable assurances that these may be attained with appropriate striving and the presence of media which facilitate their attainment are the necessary factors which conjunctively help to actualize personal and social intellectual, psychological, emotional potential and prevent self-defeating, antisocial behavior. Without such assurance and facilitating factors, the drives toward power, competence, masteries and such are subverted, twisted, expressed counterproductively, and often violently. This is the achievement of the domination of Afrikan males by their European male oppressors and hegemonists. Thus, we must conclude that the most important factor for the remediation and prevention of many problems confronting the Afrikan American and worldwide Afrikan communities is the complete liberation of these communities from White male domination and domination by any other ethnic group. This is one of the central objectives for which Afrikan males must be prepared to accomplish.

Therefore, fundamentals for the education of Afrikan American males must include:

- Early inculcation of Afrikan consciousness and identity; early development of capacities for intense and loyal social relations, networking and collective actions with the ineradicable intention or ending once and for all the control of White men and other ethnic group "pretenders to the throne" of Black oppression.

- Training in reading, math and other academic areas beginning in infancy; in the meditative, spiritual and martial arts; military arts and sciences; history, logic and philosophy; literature, art and culture; science, mathematics, technology; human sociology, psychology and relations.

- Training in how to know their true enemies and in how to express their aggressive feelings outward toward them rather than against themselves.

- Training in self-governance, government and the building of institutions, of nations, and nations-within-nations. They must study *power*, its achievement and preservation as pure subject matter with the view of equaling the power of other men and successfully defending their people against the depredations of others.

- Training and practice in group dynamics, formation and facilitating skills. They must study, understand and practice the special-interest process (e.g., lobbying, political action committees, advisory committees, coalitions), the policy-formation process (e.g., how to formulate and implement policy on larger issues, establish policy planning networks, research and study groups; how to formulate propaganda and shape public opinion and influence the lawmaking process), the candidate-selection and electoral process (e.g., learning to use the electoral rules to influence party politics, establish political parties and caucuses) and the ideology process (e.g., promulgating Afrocentrism, financing and distributing ideological, critical and policy-oriented pamphlets, articles, journals, books, etc.; influencing university and college departments; shaping opinion on foreign policy; education in economics; public interest advertising).

- Training in the very practical techniques of economically gaining control of all Afrikan local and national markets in how to wrest these markets from the hands of other exploitative ethnic groups — by any means necessary.

- Training in how to aggressively move into national and multinational business and economic circles, geopolitical and military alliances so as to be among those who determine the direction of world socioeconomic development and to no longer be the subjects of direction by others.

- Training in the achievement of technological thinking, creativity, organization, and marketing.

- Training in Afrikan values, ethics and morals which by definition are — anti-racism, anti-imperialism, anti-domination, pro-equality, pro-peace and harmony, pro-fraternity, pro-liberty, humanistic and spiritualistic.

- Training in how to create job and economic opportunities for self and others.

Specific Attitudes and Abilities

- Learn thinking, reasoning, analytical, evaluative and wisdom skills; verbal, oratorical, negotiation and persuasion skills.

- Learn to demonstrate masculinity through the mastery of formal education, technical and professional skills, occupational, romantic, marital and familial success.

- Learn to be respectful of elders, women, children and to be solicitous of others who may be in need of support.

- Learn roles of Afrikan adults and their functions in maintaining the viability and advancing the interests of the Afrikan community.

- Learn parenting and family-husbandry skills; husband-wife, parent-child communications and bonding skills.

Community-based
Strategies for Crime Prevention

Overall, criminal violence is a type of *social* encounter or interaction. It reflects various types of social attitudes and relations and therefore always occurs in some explicit or implicit social context. It always has some type of social history or related series of social antecedents. Crime has no useful meaning outside some social or ecological context. Therefore, criminality, its shapes, forms, and functions, its prevalence and incidence, is intimately related to and a social product of the social context or system in which it is manifested. Criminality cannot be understood and explained without understanding how it is induced in significant part by the structure and functionality of the social system which gives it birth and which sustains its life.

When we study criminality across various nations, societies, cultures, subcultures and classes, we note very significant differences in rates, types and other forms of crime which somehow are related to the differences between and within these social systems, strata or categories. An instructive starting point for seeking to discover the causal bases for criminality within a particular society, especially where criminality of a certain general type; e.g., violence, which tends to occur more prevalently in a particular segment of the society than others, is to look at the gross structural and social differences in that society. One may then discover certain consistent and substantial correlations between some of these differences and certain types and levels of criminality.

The United States of America is a society marred by sharp and deep differences, a nation of outstanding inequities between its various social and class groups. Some of its most important group and class inequities exist between White and Black Americans in general; between its upper, middle and working classes (largely White), and its lower, working poor and under classes (largely Black). It is these inequities which are the fertile sources of much of crime in America and its relatively higher violent incidence in the Afrikan American community, particularly in that community's lower socioeconomic strata. We can but agree with the noted criminologist Elliot Currie (1985) when he contends that:

> It isn't accidental, then, that among developed coun-
> tries, the United States is afflicted simultaneously with
> the worst rates of violent crime, the widest spread of
> income inequality, and the most severe public policies
> toward the disadvantaged. The industrial societies that
> have escaped our extremes of criminal violence tend
> either to have highly-developed public sectors with
> fairly generous systems of income support, relatively
> well developed employment policies and other cushions
> against "the forces of the market. . . ."

Currie goes on to compile evidence which demonstrates clearly "that higher homicide rates [are] linked with several measures of economic inequity and other disparities in income, nutritional consumption, education, and the like." Concentrated poverty, the single greatest risk factor, interactively combined with racism, the absence of good health services, dysfunctional schools, irrational and discriminatory employment and income policies, unresponsive and inadequate social services, provides a potent mixture of malefactors which often explodes with violent and destructive repercussions. Obviously, these factors must be markedly improved and the American social system radically reformed if the problems of Black-on-Black adolescent violence and criminality along with the other social ailments of Black America are to be cured and prevented. Therefore, the Afrikan American community must organize itself, strengthen its resolve and unflinchingly utilize all of its considerably influential economic social and political power to transform the American social system for its own communal and America's own national betterment. The Afrikan American community has demonstrated its ability to change the American landscape on a number of important occasions, most notably during the antebellum and civil war era and the 1960s. It can do so again if it chooses to do so.

**The Black American
Political Economy and Crime**

While individual, one-on-one, and group educational, preventive, remedial, rehabilitative and psychotherapeutic approaches can be effective, if effectively and appropriately applied, they do not deal directly with the large sociopolitical and socioeconomic variables which are the root causes of the largest portion of group and individual problems. Unless basic social problems engendered by a dysfunctional socioeconomic system are resolved, the strategies and activities alluded to above can only be ameliorative or provide symptomatic relief at best. They could never turn back the flood of children and adolescents with special problems so massively produced by a malfunctional social system as is current in the United States today. Therefore, broad national and community-institutional reforms are necessary (in combination with specific approaches and programs) for the meaningful prevention of Black adolescent violence and crime. Recommendations by Currie (1985) for helping to prevent crime in America may serve as an example to the type of national and community measures which may be undertaken to begin to very significantly reduce criminal violence in America and especially in the Afrikan-American community. The recommendations by Currie include the following:

- Exploration and development of intensive reha-bilitation programs for youthful offenders, preferably in local community or in a supportive institutional milieu.
- Community-based, comprehensive family support programs, emphasizing local participation and respect for cultural diversity.
- Improved family planning services and support for teenaged parents.
- Paid work leaves and more accessible child care for parents with young children, to ease the conflicts between child-rearing and work.
- High-quality, early-prevention programs for dis-advantaged children.
- Expanded community dispute-resolution programs.

- Comprehensive, locally based services for victims of domestic violence.

- Intensive job training, perhaps modeled along the lines of supported work, designed to prepare the young and the displaced for stable careers.

- Strong support for equity in pay and conditions, aimed at upgrading the quality of low-paying jobs.

- Substantial *permanent* public and public-private job creation in local communities, at wages sufficient to support a family breadwinner, especially in areas of clear and pressing social needs like public safety, rehabilitation, child care and family support.

- Universal — and generous — income support for families headed by individuals outside the paid labor force.

In addition to Currie's recommendations, major strides in eliminating or greatly reducing Black adolescent violence and crime can be made if national governmental efforts were successfully undertaken to markedly improve the social context in which many Black inner-city adolescents live today. The positive transformation of this crimogenic context, in conjunction with Afrikan-centered education and consciousness, should go far toward making the Afrikan American community violence and crime free.

We must also note that violence and criminality within the Afrikan American community not only reflect socio-economic distortions and inequalities within the larger White-dominated American social system but economic and therefore social dislocations in the Black-dominated social subsystem itself. In addition to relatively lower rates of participation in the general labor market due to historical and contemporary racism and "human capital deficits [i.e., educated, trained, skilled workers] that continued to limit qualifications of black workers. . ." (Swinton, 1990), the Afrikan American community is further impeded by its severely limited wealth and business ownership and a self-defeating consumer orientation. That is, the local ownership of portions of businesses and public corporations in the larger economy are essentially negligible given the size and the learning/spending power of this community. The Afrikan American community is virtually totally dis-invested and shamelessly economically exploited by other ethnic groups who own and control its local markets and real estate and thereby remove billions of dollars daily from its coffers, robbing it of its wealth and the concomitant power which accompanies it. The relative failure of the Afrikan American community to invest in the wealth-producing instruments offered by the general American market economy means a devastating loss of opportunities to increase its socio-economic well-being and its politico-economic power. Moreover, the alarming and overwhelming tendency of Afrikan Americans to spend huge amounts of money and consume indiscriminately with and from non-black businesses and service establishments who contribute little or nothing to their economic growth and stability, almost completely destroys that community's ability to "do for self" and use its own rather considerable potential to solve many of its problems such as Black-on-Black adolescent violence and criminality.

As observed by Swinton (1990), "These disadvantages in ownership and we may add, [spending/consumption patterns] generate the disadvantages observed in self-employment, property, and retirement income." Through its indiscriminate spending and consumer habits the Afrikan American community enriches and subsidizes the families and children of other ethnic groups, thereby helping to economically stabilize their communities, reduce their rates of violence and crime, and enhancing their accumulation of wealth and political power while dis-investing and empowering its own families and children economically, devitalizing itself, increasing its rates of violence and crime, and creating deficits in its economic and political power.

The Afrikan American community could very markedly reduce crime, violence, miseducation, poverty, etc., if it would become conscious of itself as a nation-within-a-nation, of its spending, consumption and investment patterns and organize its consciousness in ways which best serve its own material and nonmaterial interests. It must remove predatory merchants and service establishments from its internal markets and assume ownership and control of those markets; it must monitor how and how much it spends with large, national and multinational companies and the contributions these companies make to the community, its institutions and economic well-being and spend or not spend with them accordingly; it must organize itself as national and international economic network and invest its wealth in its local markets, the national markets and the international markets, especially in countries, nations and areas where Afrikan people predominate. The process of accomplishing these ends will radically and positively transform the Afrikan American/Pan Afrikan socioeconomic landscape and in its wake, transform its violent and delinquent youths into productive, prosocial community members and adults.

The approaches discussed above and related approaches, as well as new and innovative approaches derived from clear observation of the behavior of Afrikan American boys based on a thorough understanding Afrikan/Afrikan American history, culture, sociology, can be of very significant importance in reversing the violent trends now prevalent in the Afrikan American and Pan-Afrikan communities, and to prepare them to do their part in achieving the liberation of Afrikan peoples and to contribute to the liberation of Humankind as a whole.

■

Appendix

Organizational Strategies and Activities
for Preventing Black Adolescent Violence[d]

Educational Strategies: Mentoring

NAME	TARGET GROUP
Black Male Youth Project 1510 9th St., N.W. Washington DC 20001 (202) 332-0213	Males, ages 11-17
Project 2000 Morgan State University, School of Education in Urban Studies 322 Jenkins Hall, Baltimore, MD 21239 (301) 444-3275	Elementary school-age males, from single-parent, female-headed homes
Project Image 765 E. 69th St., Chicago, IL 60637 (312) 324-8700	African American males ages 8-18
Project PEACE 534 E. 69th St. 1st fl. Chicago, IL 60653 (312) 791-4768	Elementary and high school students near public housing
Project PEACE 605 N. Eutaw, St., Baltimore, MD 21201 (301) 685-8316	High-risk youth in fifth, sixth, and seventh grades
Young Men's Project 3030 W. Harrison St., Chicago, Il 60612 (312) 265-7440 6000 S. Wentworth Ave., Chicago, Il 60621 (312) 225-4433	African American males

[d] Adaptation of a list compiled by the Centers for Disease Control (CDC) 1992 (Draft).

79

Appendix

NAME	TARGET GROUP
Black Male Youth Project 1510 9th Street, N.W. Washington DC 20001 (202) 332-0213	Males, ages 11-17
Project 2000 Morgan State University of Education in Urban Studies 322 Jenkins Hall, Baltimore MD 21239 (301) 444-3275	Elementary school-age males, from single-parent, female-headed homes
Youth at Risk 3059 Fillmore St., San Francisco, CA 94123 (415) 673-0717	Youth, ages 15-20

Educational Strategies: Conflict Resolution

NAME	TARGET GROUP
Boston Conflict Resolution Program Box 271, 523 N. Broadway, Nyack, NY 10960 (914) 358-4601	Early elementary school children and teachers
Children's Creative Response to Conflict	Early elementary school children
Grant Middle School Conflict Resolution Training 2400 Grant Boulevard, Syracuse, NY 13208 (315) 435-4433	Students
Hawaii Meditation Program Univ. of Hawaii at Manoa, West Hall Annex 2, Room 222, 1776 University Ave., Honolulu, HI 96822	Students
House of Umoja Boystown 1410 N. Frazier Street, Philadelphia, PA 19131 (215) 473-5893	Potential gang members

NAME	TARGET GROUP
Resolving Conflict Creativity Program 163 Third Ave., #239 NY, NY 10003 (212) 260-6290	Children and youth in grades K-12
Santa Fe Mountain Center State of New Mexico	High risk youth First offenders
School Initiatives Program 149 Ninth Street, San Francisco, CA 94103 (415) 552-1250	Students
Urban Interpersonal Violence Injury Control Project Kansas City, Missouri	High-risk youth, usually referred through courts or social services
Violence Prevention Project 1010 Massachusetts Ave., Boston, MA 02118 (617) 534-5196	Adolescents
Voyageur Outward Bound School 500 W. Madison Street, Suite 2100, Chicago, IL 60606 (312) 715-0550	Gang members, 13-17 years of age

Educational Strategies: Training in Life and Social Skills

NAME	TARGET GROUP
Barron Assessment and Counseling Center 25 Walk Hill Street, Jamaica Plan MA 02130 (617) 469-4606	Weapon carriers
Boston Conflict Resolution Program Box 271, 523 N. Broadway, Nyack, NY 10960 (914) 358-4601	Elementary school children and teachers

Appendix

NAME	TARGET GROUP
Channeling Children's Anger 4545 42nd St. N.W. Suite 311, Washington, DC 20016 (202) 364-7111	Junior and senior students. Professionals who work with young people and their families
Chicanos por la Causa 1112 E. Buckeye Road, Phoenix, AZ 85034 (602) 257-0700	High risk youth
Children's Creative Response to Conflict [no address]	Early elementary school children
Community Youth Gang Services Project 144 S. Fetterly Ave., Los Angeles, CA 90022 (213) 632-2947	Gang members Potential gang members
Early Adolescent Helper Program 25 West 43rd Street, Rm. 620, NYC NY 10036 (212) 642-2947	Adolescents, ages 10-15
Gang Peace 32 Gaston Street, Roxbury, MA (714) 535-3722	Gang members Potential gang members
Gang Prevention and Intervention Program 1602 S. Brookhurst St., Anaheim, CA 92804 (714) 535-3722	School-age youth
Good Grief Program 295 Longwood Ave., Boston MA 02115 (617) 232-8390	Children who experience a death of a family member or friend through violence
House of Umoja Boystown 1410 N. Frazier, Philadelphia, PA 19131 (215) 473-5893	Potential gang members

NAME	TARGET GROUP
HAWK Federation Manhood Development and Training Program 155 Filbert Street, #202, Oakland, California 94607 (415) 836-3245	Adolescent African Americans
Milwaukee Public Schools P.O. Drawer, 10K, Milwaukee, WI 53201 (414) 475-8393	African American males
"OUCH" Theatre 500 N. Robert Street, Suite 220, St. Paul, MN 55101 (612) 227-9660	Elementary school children
The Paramount Plan 16400 Colorado Ave., Paramount, CA 90723 (213) 220-2140	Potential gang members
PATHS: Providing Alternative Thinking Strategies University of Washington, Seattle, WA 98195	Early elementary school children
Philadelphia Injury Prevention Program 500 S. Broad Street, Philadelphia, PA 19146 (215) 875-5661	Gang members
Project SPIRIT 600 New Hampshire Ave. N.W., Suite 650, Washington, DC 20037 (202) 333-3060	Children and parents
Santa Fe Mountain Center State of New Mexico	High-risk youth First offenders
Southeast Community Day Center School 9525 E. Imperial Highway, Downey, CA 90242 (213) 922-6821	Juvenile offenders

Appendix

NAME	TARGET GROUP
Southeastern Michigan Spinal Cord Injury System 261 Mack Avenue, Detroit, MI 48201 (313) 745-9740	High school students
Teens, Crime, and the Community National Crime Prevention Council 733 15th Street, N.W., Suite 540, Washington DC 20005 (205) 393-7141	Students
Urban Interpersonal Violence Injury Control Project Kansas City, Missouri	High-risk youth, usually referred through courts and social services
Viewpoints Training Program Center for Research on Aggression, Dept. of Psychology, P.O. Box 4348 M/C 285, Chicago, IL 60680 (312) 413-2624	Violent youth
Voyageur Outward Bound School 500 W. Madison Street, Suite 2100, Chicago, IL 60606 (312) 715-0550	Gang members, 13-17 years of age
Where Have All the Children Gone? 2051 W. Grand Boulevard, Detroit, MI 48208 (313) 895-4000	Students, 10-17 years of age
The Yale-New Haven Social Competence Promotion Program New Haven, Connecticut	Students
Young Men's Project 3030 W. Harrison St., Chicago, IL 60612 (312) 265-7440 60000 S. Wentworth Ave., Chicago, Il 60621 (312) 225-4433	African American males

84

NAME	TARGET GROUP
Youth at Risk 3059 Fillmore St., San Francisco, CA 94123 (415) 673-0717	Youth, ages 15-20
Youth Development, Inc. 1710 Centro Familiar, S.W. Albuquerque, NM 87105 (505) 831-6038	All ages (from 3-year-olds to youth in early 20s)
102nd Street Elementary School Los Angeles, California	Children who experience a death in the family member or friend through violence

Educational Strategies: Firearm Safety

NAME	TARGET GROUP
Kids + Guns = A Deadly Equation 1450 Northeast 2nd Ave., Rm. 904, Miami, FL 33132 (305) 995-1986	Students
Public Information Campaign Charlotte, N.C. police department	Public

Educational Strategies: Recreational Activities

NAME	TARGET GROUP
Challengers Boys Group 5029 S. Vermont Ave., Los Angeles, CA 90037 (213) 971-6141	Males and females ages 6-17
Chicago Commons Association 915 N. Walcott, Chicago, IL 60622 (312) 342-5330	Gang members Potential gang members

Appendix

NAME	TARGET GROUP
Community Youth Services 144 S. Fetterly Ave., Los Angeles, CA	Gang members Potential gang members
House of Umoja Boystown 1410 N. Frazier St. Philadelphia, PA 19131	Potential gang members
Santa Fe Mountain Center State of New Mexico	High-risk youth First offenders
Urban Interpersonal Violence Injury Control Project Kansas City, Missouri	High-risk youth, usually referred through courts or social services
Youth Development, Inc. 1710 Centro Familiar, S.W., Albuquerque, NM 87105 (505) 831-6038	All ages (from 3-year-olds to youth in early 20s)

Environmental Strategies: Work Opportunities

NAME	TARGET GROUP
Chicago Commons Association 917 N. Walcott, Chicago, IL 60622 (312) 342-5330	Gang members Potential gang members
Chicano por la Causa	Juvenile offenders
Community Youth Gang Services 144 S. Fetterly Ave., Los Angeles CA 90022 (213) 266-4264	Gang members Potential gang members
Early Adolescent Program Helper 25 West 43rd Street, Room 620 NY, NY 10036 (212) 643-2947	Adolescents, ages 10-15

NAME	TARGET GROUP
Gang Peace 32 Gaston Street, Roxbury, MA (416) 443-7391	Gang members Potential gang members
Southeast Community Day Center School 9525 East Imperial Highway, Downey, CA 90242	Juvenile offenders
Youth Development, Inc. 1710 Centro Familiar, S.W. Albuquerque, NM 87105	All ages (from 3-year-olds to youth in early 20s)

Environmental Strategies: Therapeutic Activities

NAME	TARGET GROUP
House of Umoja Boystown 1410 N. Frazier St., Philadelphia, PA 19131 215 473-5893	Potential gang members
Philadelphia Injury Prevention Program 500 S. Broad Street, Philadelphia, PA 19146 (215) 875-5661	Gang members
Save Our Sons and Daughters 453 Martin Luther Boulevard, Detroit, MI 48201 (303) 833-3030	Parents Public
Violence Prevention Project 1010 Massachusetts Ave., Boston, MA 02118 (617) 534-5196	Adolescent

Bibliography

Bell, C. and Jenkins, E. 1990. "Preventing Black Homicide" in *The State of Black America 1990*. New York: National Urban League, pp.143-155.

Centers for Disease Control (CDC), U.S. Department of Health and Human Resources. 1991. *Guidelines for Prevention of Youth Violence: A Community Approach* (Draft Copy), Atlanta.

Conger, J. and Miller, W. 1966. *Personality, Social Class, and Delinquency*. New York: Wiley.

Cruse, H. 1987. *Plural But Equal: A Critical Study of Blacks and Minorities and American's Plural Society*. New York: William Morrow/Quill.

Currie, E. 1985. *Confronting Crime: An American Challenge*. New York: Pantheon Books.

Dietz, P. 1987. "Patterns in Human Violence" in R.E. Hales and A.J. France (eds.), *Psychiatric Update: The American Psychiatric Association Annual Review, Vol. 5*. Washington, D.C.: American Psychiatric Press.

Federal Bureau of Investigation. 1987. *Crime in the United States: 1986*. Washington, D.C.: U.S. Department of Justice.

Fenichel, O. 1945. *The Psychoanalytical Theory of Neuroses*. New York: W.W. Norton.

Garrow, D. 1981. *The FBI and Martin Luther King, Jr*. New York: Penguin Books.

Gilmore, D. 1990. *Manhood in the Making: Cultural Concepts of Masculinity*. New Haven: Yale University Press.

Glueck, S. and Glueck, E. 1968. *Delinquents and Nondelinquents in Perspective*. Cambridge, MA: Harvard University Press.

Glueck, S. and Glueck, E. 1950. *Unraveling Juvenile Delinquency*. Cambridge, MA: Harvard University Press.

Goldstein, A. Sprafkin, R, Gershaw, N. and Klein, 1980. *Skillstreaming the Adolescent: A Structured Learning*

Approach to Teaching Prosocial Skills. Champaign, Illinois: Research Press.

Gough, H. 1948. "A Sociological Theory of Psychopathy" in *American Journal of Sociology, 53*: 356-366.

Hilliard A., Payton-Stewart, L. & Williams, L., eds. 1990. *Infusion of African and African American Content in the School Curriculum.* Proceeding of the First Nation Conference, October 1989. Morristown, NJ: Aaron Press.

Hirschi, T. & Hindelang, M. 1977. "Intelligence and Delinquency: A Revisionist View" in *American Sociological Review, 42*, 571-587.

Hirschi, T. 1969. *Causes of Delinquency.* Berkeley, CA: University of California Press.

Lowen, A. 1958. *The Language of the Body.* New York: Collier-Macmillan.

McCord, W. and McCord, J. 1964. *The Psychopath: An Essay on the Criminal Mind.* Princeton, NJ: Van Nostrand.

Millon, T. 1969. *Modern Psychopathology: A Biosocial Approach to Maladaptive Learning and Functioning.* Philadelphia: W.B. Saunders Co.

Reich, W. 1945. *Character Analysis.* 3rd ed. New York: Farrar, Straus & Giroux.

"Report of the Commissioner's Task Force on Minorities: Equity and Excellence." July 1989. *A Curriculum of Inclusion.*

Riordan, C. 1990. *Girls and Boys in School: Together or Separate?* New York: Teachers College Press.

Robins, R., Murphy, G., Woodruff, R., Jr. & King, L. 1971. "The Adult Psychiatric Status of Black Schoolboys" in *Archives of General Psychiatry, 24*: 338-345.

Rosenberg, M., and Mercy, J. 1986. "Homicide: Epidemiologic Analysis at the National Level" in *Bulletin of the New York Academy of Medicine, 62*: 376-399.

"Secretary's Task Force on Black and Minority Health" in *Report of the Secretary's Task Force on Black and Minority Health, Volume 1, Executive Summary.* 1985. Washington, DC: U.S. Dept. of Health and Human Services.

Selwan, R. In Press. *Making A Friend.* Chicago: University of Chicago Press.

Sills, D., ed. 1968. "Assimilation" in *International Encyclopedia of the Social Sciences.* Vol. 1. New York: Macmillan/Free Press.

Swinton, D. 1989. "Economic Status of Black Americans During the 1980s: A Decade of Limited Progress" in *The State of Black America 1990.* N.Y.: National Urban League, Inc. pp. 25-52.

Wallace, A. 1970. *Culture and Personality.* 2nd ed. New York: Random House.

West, D. and Farrington, D. 1973. *Who Becomes Delinquent?* London: Heinemann Education Books.

Willi, J. 1982. *Couples in Collusion: The Unconsciousness Dimension in Partner Relationships.* Claremont, CA: Hunter House.

Wilson, Amos. 1990. *Black-on-Black Violence: The Psycho-dynamics of Black Self-Annihilation in Service of White Domination.* New York: Afrikan World InfoSystems.

Wilson, J. and Herrnstein, R. 1985. *Crime and Human Nature.* New York: Simon & Schuster/Touchstone.

Index

Index

Brief Profiles of Five Other Books by Amos Wilson

ck-on-Black Violence: The Psychodynamics Black Self-Annihilation in Service of White mination represents a distinct milestone in ninology and Afrikan studies. It theorizes that operational existence of Black-on-Black lence in the U.S.A. is psychologically and nomically mandated by the White American-ninated status quo. The criminalization of the ck American male is a psychopolitically ;ineered process geared to maintain depend-y and relative powerlessness of the Afrikan erican and Pan-Afrikan communities. Wilson, ond blaming the victimizer, exposes the chosocial and intrapsychical dynamics of ck-on-Black criminality. PB. Pages: 224

eprint for Black Power: A Moral, Economic 1 Political Imperative for the 21st Century ails a master plan for the power revolution essary for Black survival in the 21st century. eprint... illuminates that Afrikan Americans e home nearly $500 billion yearly of the lions they generate yet retain merely 5% of ; income. Viewed as a nation their economy uld be 8th or 9th largest in the world! Wilson ues that were the Afrikan American commu-y to view itself as a de facto nation and orga-e as such, then its scourges of poverty, mployment, crime, mis-education, consum-m, mis-leadership and powerlessness would drastically reduced. He deconstructs and egitimates the U.S. governmental and power e structures, debunks ethnocentrism, global erial capitalism and their portent for Blacks, roundly castigates the ineptitude of Black ophantic religious and political leadership. eprint warns Black obsolescence in the ning millennium! It mandates and instructs ring, radical approaches and opportunities true Black Power globally. PB. Pages: 912

akening the Natural Genius of Black ldren. Afrikan children are naturally preco-s and gifted. They begin life with a "natural d start." Intelligence is not fixed at birth. re is clear evidence that the quality of chil-n's educational experiences during infancy early childhood are substantially related to r measured intelligence, academic achieve-nt and social behavior. Wilson reveals the y routines, child-rearing practices, parent-d interactions, games and play materials,

parent training and pre-school programs which have made demonstrably outstanding and lasting differences in the intellectual, academic and social performance of Afrikan American children. PB. Pages: 144

The Developmental Psychology of the Black Child

- Are Black and White children the same?
- Is the Black child a White child who happens to be "painted" Black?
- Are there any significant differences in the mental and physical development of Black and White children?
- Do Black parents socialize their children to be inferior to White children?

This pioneering book looks at these and other related controversial questions from an Afrikan perspective. The topics of growth, development and education are scholarly explored.

PB. Pages: 216

The Falsification of Afrikan Consciousness is a double feature. The first, *The Role of Eurocentric Historiography in the European Oppression of Afrikan People*, was among the first contemporary analyses which delineated the role Eurocentric history writing plays in rationalizing European oppression of Afrikan peoples and in the falsifi-cation of Afrikan consciousness. It explicates why we should study history; how history writing shapes the psychology of peoples and individuals; how Eurocentric history as mythol-ogy creates historic amnesia in Afrikans in order to rob them of the material, mental, social and spiritual wherewithal for overcoming poverty and oppression.

Part II, *Eurocentric Political Dogmatism: Its Relationship to Mental Health Misdiagnosis of Afrikan Peoples*, advances that the alleged mental and behavioral maladaptiveness of oppressed Afrikan peoples is a political-economic necessity for the maintenance of White domination and imperialism. It indicts the Eurocentric mental health establishment for entering into collusion with the Eurocentric political establishment to oppress and exploit Afrikan peoples by officially sanctioning egregious practices through its misdiagnosing, mislabeling, and mistreating of Afrikan peoples' behavioral reactions to their oppression and their efforts to win their freedom and independence. PB. Pages: 152

To Order *Blueprint For Black Power*

Blueprint For Black Power: *A Moral, Economic and Political Imperative for the 21st Century*
ISBN # 1-879164-06-X   SOFT BOUND   **Price $38.00**

(If ordering via mail please complete this order form and mail with remittance to the address provided below):

Title & Quantity of books	Unit Price	Total
	Subtotal	$_____
	8.25% Sales Tax (NY only)	$_____
	8.25% Sales Tax (TN only)	$_____
	*Shipping & Handling	$_____
	Total Order	$_____

*Shipping & Handling depend on the number of books bought — see below
1 Book $5.95   2-5 Books $10.00   6-10 Books $16.00
For orders over 10 books, just call customer service at the phone number below

Other Books by Amos N. Wilson	ISBN Number	Price
Black-on-Black Violence	1-879164-00-0	$15.00
The Falsification of Afrikan Consciousness	1-879164-02-7	$10.95
Awakening the Natural Genius of Black Children	1-879164-01-9	$ 9.95
Understanding Black Adolescent Male Violence	1-879164-03-5	$ 7.95
The Developmental Psychology of the Black Child	686-24183-5	$10.95

*Shipping & Handling depend on the number of books bought — see below
1 Book $4.95   2-5 Books $8.95   6-10 Books $12.95

To Order by Telephone call 718 462-1830
Http://www.ominara@aol.com
To Order by Mail:
Just fill out the information below and send this page with your remittance to:

Order Dept.
Afrikan World InfoSystems
743 Rogers Avenue, Suite 6
Brooklyn, New York 11226

Name

Address

City   State   Zip

Certified Check/Money Order enclosed for   Pay to: **Afrikan World InfoSystems**